The
CORPORATE
HIPPIE

KIMBERLY ADAMS

The
CORPORATE
HIPPIE

Praise for *The Corporate Hippie* and the Teachings of Kimberly Adams

"Kim's heart-led approach to building teams is where all businesses should be heading. There has been transformational Innovation in my leadership approach, and I believe this book is the manual for anyone hiring, building, and leading teams!"

—Dave Ferrera, Author of *Innovation in Translation*

"The Corporate Hippie is a raw story about being human and shows how *growing up* is a lifelong journey. This book gives you the power to discover and nurture your inner beauty and to live the life *you* want—full of everything you ever dreamed. My favorite part is how to use your thoughts to connect with others, build lasting relationships and grow exponentially. A *must read.*"

—Ann Piper, Kim's former VP at YuMe

"Kim's positive intentions have transformed my every day and I could not be more grateful. MAGIC is right!"

—Lynsey Skoch, former employee at YuMe,
and 1st hire working under these guiding principles

"Kim has the unique ability to find and cultivate talent by using her inner compass to compassionately motivate and inspire her peers. We live in a culture that promotes and rewards relentless dedication to one's craft, often leading to burnout and numerous personal sacrifices. Kim takes a different approach. By encouraging and focusing on the emotional and physical health of her employees, Kim creates an environment that yields the greatest and highest outcome for all. With a self-care first mentality, I was able to bring my best and brightest self to work every day. In this safe space I saw tremendous personal and professional growth, which I could have never achieved without Kim's guidance. Companies take notice. This is the way of the future."

—Katie Flora, former employee at YuMe

"I met Kim Adams five years ago, and she has had a profound impact on my life. She was my boss and had extremely high expectations with regards to business and performance. However, she had higher expectations pertaining to self-care. Self-care looks different to different people. For me, it includes meditation, prayer, choosing positivity and manifesting the things I want in my life. My relationship with Kim has allowed me to recognize the importance of taking care of myself and how that translates into a better life for myself, my family and my job performance."

–Lauren Albin, former employee at YuMe

"There are certain people that come into your life that you just know are truly special, for me this is Kim! Kim's infectious personality and zest for life, yet calming aura, has helped me immeasurably in getting out of my own comfort zone, trusting, and believing in my own being. She inspires me to continue to follow my intuition and my heart's truth as I learn and discover my own spiritual journey along with her intuitive guidance and knowledge. For this and so many other reasons I am so grateful and blessed to have her in my life."

–Diane Boudreau, Seeker and supporter of Kim's vision

"Kim has taught and inspired me to dream, manifest, and heal....always leading with her intuition with what she knows to be true. There have been so many wonderful things come into her life by living this way. I'm grateful for the beautiful changes in my own life by learning from her. Kim's passion and fire for sharing this are inspiring and infectious!"

–Susan H., longtime friend

"Kim's style is self-care 1st and the rest takes care of itself. Kim taught me an incredible amount about myself by simply sharing her personal journey. This has impacted the way I do business, the way I spend time with my family and my own self-care. I've taken giant leaps with Kim's support!

–Lindsey Dobbs, former employee at YuMe

"Thank you, Kim, for being so supportive. You are truly the best and I am so grateful for you. Personally, professionally, mentally and spiritually, you've really been a blessing to me!"

–Kerry O'Dorisio, former employee at YuMe

"What a pleasure it is to know Kim Adams. Not only have we had a successful business relationship, but over the years she has also become one of my dearest friends. Vision and Authenticity make Kim unique in business and in building lasting relationships. She sees the bigger picture by always putting client needs first. One of things I love most about Kim is no matter the situation (professionally or personally), she makes things happen. Not only has she made things happen for my clients, but she always took the time to get to know each person. Kim has also helped me with my personal growth. I've learned so much from her about how to be in the workplace, as well as how to just be myself and how to be open to life. It's rare that you come across a person like Kim. She shines bright. And I'm extremely lucky to have her unconditional love and support!"

–LaDonna Miller, former client from The Richards Group

"I couldn't be more grateful for Kim's guiding light. She has taught me the importance of self-care, positive thinking, BIGGER thinking, and truly manifesting how to get what you want in life. With her help, I am absolutely living my best life, and I know there's even more to come!"

–Jennifer McCallum former employee at YuMe

DEDICATIONS

To Mom, Dad and Stepmom—you've each loved me, laughed and cried with me. Thank you for being a part of my journey to remembering what my soul came here to do.

To my partner and love of my life, Dave Ferrera.
Thank you for loving, accepting, and supporting me exactly as I am. I love that we are manifesting our BIG DREAMS together and creating our own MAGIC!

TABLE OF CONTENTS

SPECIAL THANKS

Here's a big thanks from a woman who started writing this book in Texas and finished it in California.

To my partner Dave who spends every moment of every day making my heart and soul feel at home.

To Diane Ferrera Boudreau for your unwavering support.

Thank you to my other family members including Marla and Pierce, to my friends, my healers, my teachers, my beloved bonus kids (Tyler, Taylor, Conor, Natalia, and Emilio)...I love each of you so much!

Maybe the most important thanks to God, my Angels, Guides and Cheerleaders on the other side for guiding me through my intuition...
What are we doing next?!

Next, thank you, Carrie Glenn, for being the best editor and helping me complete those final steps of getting my book ready for people to actually read.
Thank you for being a cheerleader for my book.

Most of all, thank you, Dear Reader.
I hope that you manifest the shit out of
your life, and thank you for being an
unwitting partner in helping me manifest
this magical manuscript!
It is written for you.

INTRODUCTION

I've heard people say, "Oh, he can't change," or "Don't expect her to change," and sadly, that's true for many.

I'm proud to say that doesn't describe the author, Kim Adams, her Dad, or me—her stepmom. We've grown up together and we've all changed a lot! And that's what Kim's book is about: finding your worth and making changes.

When I first met her over 30 years ago, I was a friend of her father's. They came over to my house for dinner, and it wasn't until years later that I would hear her describe that first meeting.

Kim had been attracted to my Mercedes convertible and diamond rings. She was impressed by my successful career and the fact that I had a house of my own. She said to herself, "I want to get me some of that!"

Kim had seen a different type of woman than what she was used to seeing. She'd met a woman she could become.

She also met a woman who shared a deep, heartfelt connection with others above all that superficial stuff. She found wisdom and great advice, and woman who cares so much for her. She discovered a woman who understands that, yes! It *is* all about the stuff! Though, not the material possessions I'd acquired as one might assume, but rather, the stuff *inside*—how people feel about you, not the things you have.

At eighteen-years-old, and for many years after, I would witness Kim's emotional turmoil. It seemed when we talked over lunch or dinner, she always ended up crying, even in restaurants. At first, it felt uncomfortable because I didn't want strangers to think her dad and I were the cause. Then, I realized that the conversations we were having (which were about life in general and how she was raised) were much more important than what others thought about them. Over the next thirty-four years, we developed a great appreciation for one another's depth.

Three years ago found us crying in front of strangers yet again. It was our trip to Miraval, a wellness spa in Tucson (and very generous gift from Kim and my husband for my 65th birthday). We were expressing our admiration and gratitude for one another during our first session. Neither Kim nor I tried to hold back those tears. How far we'd come!

Our time at Miraval got me started practicing meditation, and when we left, Kim loaded an app onto my iPhone for Oprah and Deepak Chopra's free meditation series, "Making Every Moment Matter."

Because of Kim, meditation has become a part of what I do each day. It is one of her self-care tools. I can even close my eyes and go back to Miraval. I remember the feeling of *hanging in the silks*, of being massaged while floating on water, of beating large exercise balls with drumsticks. Meditation has changed my life.

Some relationships constantly evolve, and you learn new things and expand new ideas. That's Kim. Always searching, discovering, encouraging, and challenging others to join in. She has become one of my shining lights in life. She makes me smile when I think about her, and she especially makes me smile when I'm with her.

She can swoop in and get things done and have fun doing it! Kim has a very generous spirit and strong desire to share what she has learned and discovered. She thrives on lifting burdens and worries and replacing them with spa treatments and emotional tools!

She emanates infectious feelings of joy. She's released. Open.

Kim is someone who enhances your life, surprises you, and opens up a new avenue of thinking, one that's filled with signs. Her book shows that one of the biggest things we can do is recognize the signs that come our way. There are no accidents. The more we see, the more connected we will be. We become more and more aware of what we want.

Bottom line is how proud I am of Kim for becoming a happy and healthy person. She didn't know what that was at age 18. She still didn't totally know what being happy and healthy was in her early thirties or when she got married the first time, but she was always working at figuring it out.

And she never gave up. She knows it now and wants to share it with you.

Kim is directly responsible for helping me make two big changes in my life. One is the daily meditation. The second and most incredible change of all, is getting a dog.

Kim repeatedly told her father and me, "Ya'll should get a dog."

I resisted. I liked my life the way it was. I didn't like messing up the house. I liked being able to go and do without being tied down. But then, her dad named our imaginary dog Gracie.

This went on for at least a year. We'd talk about what it would be like to have a dog. I talked to breeders, went to dog romps, and talked to owners.

One day I was sitting at lunch with friends after a round of golf, and Kim's dad called.

"Well, I bought that puppy."

"You did what?"

I had given him the names of breeders, and he had called them and decided to buy our puppy, Gracie.

When I got off the phone, one friend said, "Oh no… You don't want to do that."

Another told a story about her puppy eating the wallpaper.

We had to pick Gracie up that Sunday when I was supposed to be playing in an annual golf tournament, so I had to cancel.

Oh my gosh, she hasn't even moved in yet, and already she's screwing up my golf!

Now, it's been years. And I wouldn't take any amount of money for Gracie. She is the love of my life. I've never felt this way about anything or anyone. So . . . I was open—a little—to the idea of a dog.

The nudges finally worked their magic. It is a change in my life that I thank God for every day.

And to Kim, a big, exuberant, slobbery, "Thank you," for knowing we needed a dog! Pure love and joy!

Big life changes like this start with simple awareness, the work you put into knowing what you want, and the openness of how you go after it. For Kim and me, I'll give the credit to a great counselor for helping us discover the beginning of our awareness and sharpen the tools needed for real change.

Her name is Donna LeBlanc.

She got us started years ago and worked with our entire family. She told me she has never worked with anyone as dedicated as my husband has been to raising awareness of personal issues with his children.

I have now been married to Kim's dad for over 32 years and am grateful that Kim, her sister, and brother have all helped change me into a person with a dog and a dedication to grow up together, to stay together, and work through the challenges.

So, can we change? You bet we can! And as we do, how fabulous it is to learn from your adult children, *positive turnabout is fair play!*

–Cheryl Holmes-Adams, Kim's Stepmomma

Everything is energy.
Match the frequency of
the reality you want
and you cannot help
but get that reality. It
can be no other way.
This is no philosophy.
This is physics.

Albert Einstein

Chapter 1

YOU CAN'T MAKE THIS SH!T UP!

The Princess and the Frog

*O*nce in a lifetime, the right love comes along. It's beautiful. It's perfect. It's epic. Until it crashes and burns right before your eyes. Absolute heartbreak and gut-wrenching devastation.

When this had happened to me in the past, as you might imagine, it would throw me into a tailspin. Besides the pain of lost love, I doubted my instincts, doubted my judgment, doubted my faith. I chased after each dream as it slipped away, knowing that the tighter I clasped, the faster it fled, but I was unable to stop myself until complete and utter ruin.

Not this time.

When Dave and I broke up, it was different. Maybe because I was different. I had evolved from being the girl who had her shit together in every aspect except when it came to love. With Dave, I had entered into our relationship as a whole woman. And boy, did we ever connect!

It was a deep soul, energy connection like nothing I'd ever felt before. He was my perfect complement, and I, his. I fell in love with his children. Nothing could convince me that we would ever be apart. I knew that we were meant to be. Dave was the one.

So, it kind of sucked that after waiting a lifetime to find the love of my life, we broke up after only a year. It was just like all those other heartbreaks. Except that it wasn't. I did something for the first time in a love relationship. I went deep within for all the answers.

This time, my meditating, my seeking, listening to my Inner Guru, and being on my spiritual path, all of this kicks in when I needed it most. This time, I trust the Universe and keep faith that everything's going to turn out for my best and highest, with or without Dave.

I don't try to cling to Dave, nor do I try to chase him. I don't try to change his mind or force an outcome. Instead, I use the spiritual tools that I've been using for years to succeed in my career. Instead, I use flow and trust.

I handle it with grace and self-care. I engage my Inner Guru and do surprisingly well. I keep praying for the best and highest. I have this *inner knowing*. I see my life, and I feel it. While I stand ready to accept whatever life brought me, I also believe that there is a chance Dave and I can end up together. Still, I don't obsess or go into denial or try to win him back.

I simply ask. I go down to the beach with my sister to meditate. We sit in the cool sand, waves splashing along the shore, the smell of the sea washing over us. We meditate to Oprah and Deepak Chopra, and this is when I ask.

I pray to God, to the Universe, to Divine Source for a sign from my Angels. I ask for a sign. If Dave and I are going to end up together, would God please show me a frog? Of course, I'm not really thinking of the whole frog-turning-into-a-prince thing or fairytales or anything like that. The frog just happens to be the first thing that pops into my head. Then, I wait for a spiritual sign, and boy do I get one.

The next morning my mom is asking me to turn on a specific movie. I do. Then, as I'm about to walk out to the beach, this big ass ribbiting frog is suddenly center screen. I stop and stare, thinking *no f'ing way!* Three days later, I'm going up the escalator at Neiman Marcus, and there I see this ginormous ceramic frog with a big crown on its head.

In that moment, I have my answer. I know, I simply know, that Dave is my prince, and a sense of calm washes over me.

Days go by, then weeks, then months. Nothing is happening. In the past, I would've normally started panicking and doubting. Instead, I'm still filled with this knowing and calm. I'm finally at a place in my growth where I've learned to accept when the Universe chooses silence or even another path.

So, I decide four months into this whole breakup thing that it's time for me to move forward with or without Dave. It's not an act of impatience or uncertainty. I just know that time is precious, and life is meant to be lived.

It's time to release Dave, to let him go.

I set aside some me-time, get quiet, and light a white candle. I say a prayer, asking for my soulmate, my true love, to come to me in divine timing. I meditate on this and accept the flow of the divine.

As I'm going to bed, I hop on Facebook to see how the world is doing. I see a post from Dave's sister, and it's a picture of—you guessed it! She's posted a picture of a frog! My heart quickens, and I'm staring at that frog so hard that I hardly even hear the incoming message.

It's a text. From Dave.

I read the words, "I'm in Dallas...I love you!" He has felt the energy of my letting go, and in seconds, he's acting.

It's magic!

Now, years later, we're still together. I've left my home state of Texas after 51 years and am living happily in sunny southern California, happily loving Dave. Believing and moving were my acts of self-love and faith. I have finally begun to know my worth, something that few of us do but is so very important to all growth, all success, all joy. Knowing that we are worthy is everything.

When all my friends thought I was crazy and questioned my reality, when his silence said it was over, I simply trusted. I knew with my inner knowing that we would be together, and it only took a couple of frogs to set everything back into motion.

You just can't make this shit up!

******

Why the love story? Why start a book about being a Corporate Hippie with a personal story about love? It's a fair question.

Having written this book during the COVID-19 pandemic, we've all seen how our business and personal lives are becoming more and more integrated. Now with Zoom calls, we are literally letting the people we work with into every aspect of our lives. Especially our most vulnerable parts.

We're showing our families, our dogs, our kitties, and our homes on these video calls. We're showing our rooms, our walls and windows, our bookcases, and our décor. We're showing the food we cook and the wine we drink, the kids running through the room, and our partners coming in unexpectedly. We're wearing no makeup. We're sporting our Lululemons and authentic selves. Heck! Some of us are even getting caught on Zoom using the bathroom or walking out in our boxers. *Oops!* We really are letting it all hang out. Thus, the love story.

It's been a long time coming, this shift. Many of us are seeing that we can no longer operate in these vacuums, these silos, and this is why our book starts out with a love story. As different as each of us are, we are also the same in many ways and want the same things. We all have goals, desires, and dreams, so why would we treat the people we work with differently than someone in our family?

I propose that the only way corporate America and business around the globe will be able to move forward is to operate out of principles of compassion, love, and kindness. It's time to remove toxicity from corporate America. Hitting on the assistant or using sex, racism, or anything that marginalizes entire cultural groups simply cannot stand any longer. I also propose that the integration of body, mind, and spirit in the workplace has never been a more important topic in our lives.

It starts with being a whole person, fully integrated at home, at work, and in all aspects of our lives. It's no longer enough to be a *nice person* only to turn around and treat our employees like shit. It also starts with accepting that our new norm includes Zoom calls with colleagues, with employees, and even with strangers. That's why it's now important to be mindful of the energy we are bringing into people's homes and to be watchful of the energy they bring into ours.

Our opening love story also tells us that everything in life can work through the power of using the spiritual principles when we let it. In this book, we'll delve into how we can each create our own magic in our careers, our love lives, our relationships, *everything!* We'll also explore many more examples of all the stuff that we can't make up, and we'll see how to create your own magic as a Corporate Hippie.

To do this, we'll first examine our view of hippies.

Hippies.

When my parents heard the title of this book, they rolled their eyes. And this is completely understandable! Hippies have long been synonymous with hangin' out in Birkenstocks and tie-dye while smokin' weed, doing hard drugs, and getting some free loving all day long. Stick it to the man, stick it to work, stick it to anyone who doesn't understand.

I ask you, is it crazy to think that today might be the day we challenge this stigma?

Today's hippie, especially today's *Corporate Hippie*, is a far cry from the hippie of yesteryears.

Today's Corporate Hippie is a spiritually enlightened person who brings an evolved way to work. Today's Corporate Hippie, whether a man or woman, is rejecting the not-so-distant past's *good ole boys club* way of doing business. She is always moving towards more fluidity at work where the partnership between employer and employee is mutually beneficial and where both can achieve financial and personal goals without taking advantage of the other.

Today's Corporate Hippie is a lightworker, which means she devotes her life to being a bright light in this world. She is an instrument of foundational change in corporate America, bringing a new era of how to work in this coming age of Aquarius. She fully understands and employs transformational leadership by leading with her heart. She understands basic principles of treating employees and partners not as a means to increase the organization's bottom line, but rather as an honored extension of her spiritual family. She knows that everyone benefits more (herself and her company included) from paying higher wages and considering the needs of her employees.

The Corporate Hippie isn't just a person; it's a movement, a way to work, and a way to lead after the life-altering changes most of us experienced in 2020.

The best part about the Corporate Hippie movement is all the stuff that you simply cannot even *try* to make up. For example, our bodies send us signs, not only to protect us but also to enrich us. Then, there are those golden opportunities that fall into our laps. That feeling we get when we're driving and just miss an accident, or when we make the perfect, intuition-based business decision.

Magic happens in the life of every Corporate Hippie every single day, sometimes even every hour or every minute. Because in an instant, we can change our lives, our businesses, our relationships, our every circumstance! Isn't this the way with magic? There are no limits other than the ones we set.

While most people go through their existence reacting to life's circumstances, others tap into the magical power all around them. They use this power to create and manifest magic in their careers, their personal and social circles, and their family lives. It's all intertwined, and we are powerfully magical creatures.

Whether you're a business owner, CEO, employee, entrepreneur, nonprofit executive, volunteer, homemaker, or parent, when you're a Corporate Hippie, you are plugged into a higher vibration.

You wake up feeling refreshed, energetic, and ready to meet the day. You're surrounded by love however that looks—a husband, a wife, a lover, your children, grandchildren, parents, your siblings, besties, roomies, a good book, *your cat*. Most importantly, you're filled with self-love, and it is this love that powers your manifesting.

You are content and grateful, yet at the same time, still hungry and eager for more.

You feel the infinite, magical, and remarkable events and opportunities that are coming your way, and you're filled with amazement again and again as you remember that from now on, you *never* have to struggle to let them into your life. By trusting your intuition and following the Universe's guidance, you're discovering that you absolutely *can* manifest your wildest dreams.

Because you now live a transformative life. Your business is booming, and your personal life is brimming with positivity, and your cup runneth over.

All because you said, "yes." You said, *yes* to your decision to change, to move, and to grow. You said *yes* to allowing yourself to cry and to laugh, to speak your truth, and most of all to love with your whole, entire heart. You said *yes* to choosing uncomfortable and by choosing to stretch rather than to remain atrophied by disbelief or fear.

You said *yes*.

You also feel the shift.

You know that it's time to change what's happening in corporate America. You know that this will only come from the leaders who step up and refuse the status quo.

Could you be one of the next heart-led managers just beginning your Corporate Hippie journey?

You're the reason for writing this book, and my promise to you is that within these pages, you'll discover effective methods for becoming a powerful manifestor. You'll see how regular people just like you and me bring more business into our companies and impact more lives when we choose to orchestrate our narrative. You'll find simple ways to summon success—and more than you could ever even imagine. Not only at work but also in life.

No matter where you are in your journey, whether you're a baby seeker, a mid seeker, or if you're a Quantum Seeker, you will find techniques to help you use your thoughts to connect with others, build stronger relationships, and grow exponentially.

Most importantly, this book is here to remind you that you are worthy.

You are important.

You are special.

There is no one else on the planet like you…heck, you're the reason why I decided to write this book. You're why I started my motivational speaking and consulting career. You're why I started my @ManifestwithKim Instagram page, where I post hope and magic and self-love.

Your needs and your desires matter because they were never random. Your wants are a part of your makeup, and the filling of them helps to create an even stronger and more beautiful world for all of us, not just you.

Yes, it may seem crazy, but getting your wants and needs filled never has to be at the expense of another. You never have to step on someone else to achieve your goals or take something away to get what you need.

Basically, when you get what you want, you are advancing the entire Universe. How's that for worthy?

I promise to introduce you to the power of intentions, allowing magic, and trusting the Universe. I'll encourage you to uncover your intuition, which is your God-given GPS, or as I like to call it, your *Inner Guru* (yes, you'll hear words like Guru, Angels, and spirit guides). Whatever we call it, this can transform your business, your relationships, and your everyday life.

Magic is here for everyone, and you can begin in an *instant*. Magic is the result of setting powerful intentions that directly influence the course of your life in small and large ways. Magic is not spouting spells or creating curses. It's not wands and cloaks. Magic is knowing that there are supernatural forces such as spirit guides, angels, and signs at our disposal. Using these powerful forces allows you to illuminate your daily path and life journey. Magic allows you to truly align with what your soul came here to do.

As you begin trusting your Inner Guru, the Universe begins divinely attracting your heart's desires. This means that you'll find yourself *naturally* beginning to want those things that are good for you. You *naturally* begin to attract all the things, the people, and the circumstances that are for your best and highest while repelling those things that are not in alignment. You begin to achieve those short term and long term goals because the act of alignment is bringing the magic.

The best way to begin is by using the many tools available to help you tap into your Inner Guru. Spiritual tools such as faith, stillness, and listening to your intuition and God-given GPS system. The good news is that in this book, we go over several of these tools so that you can master using them to create your magic. The even better news is that all of us already know how to use these tools because they are part of our makeup. It's just that many of us have forgotten.

But our souls haven't.

Each of our souls has come here to do its work. Our soul remembers how to listen, how to align, and how to manifest. Now it's just up to us practice using the tools so that we free up some of this magic for ourselves. Once we do, we can experience asking for something and then finding it. We can experience needing a miracle and then receiving it. We can experience clarity, success, happiness, and an overall sense of knowing and trusting that everything will be okay.

We create the world in which we want to live, and though we do still face many challenges, struggles, and even devastation, heartbreak, and deep loss, we do so with strength, knowing that the magic is still here, standing at the ready.

This brings me to you.

Can I guarantee that you will read this book and instantly (or ever, for that matter) become a magic manifestor? Unfortunately, no, I cannot.

Your work is personal, and you are the only one who can guarantee the results and benefits you'll receive. Only you know how far removed you are from remembering how to use the tools and gifts that you were born with. Only you can know how to trust your instincts, how to listen, to ask, and to receive.

However, I do believe that the ultimate power is in our thoughts, and when we apply our thoughts to our own betterment, we can achieve anything. Will this apply to you? It is my deepest wish (even without the guarantee of such success) that you will practice using these tools and begin manifesting your best and most magical life!

So, what will you get from reading this book? As I said, I can't promise specific results, but I can promise that you will learn a lot about yourself and how rewarding it can be to begin trusting your inner spiritual badass diva! The more you trust your Inner Guru, your inner GPS System, the more your energy will begin vibrating at a much higher frequency.

This can open the doors to getting what you really, deeply want. You may find that it gets easier to let go of chasing and stop using force to attract all the money, joy, and success you desire. Instead, it may become more natural to focus on *allowing* these in. So, you become more open to letting everything flow, allowing some things to flow away from you, and others to flow to you.

You may notice that you begin naturally attracting the *Rockstars* in your company. Rockstars who are magically and divinely aligned with your goals and dreams. They seem to have the power to help you take your business to its next level, scale your success, and trim the challenges. You might start attracting more like-minded team members, employees, business partners, and yes, even love into your life.

You might also attract your perfect clients and customers because you'll learn to intentionally ask for there to be mutual benefits for your business and clients.

You'll gain skills that, when applied and practiced, can help you develop your dedication to self-care, which is paramount to unlocking all the other magic in your life.

You'll discover simple practices around stillness (yes, the dreaded word: mediation) and ways to unharness its potential. Stillness is your superpower. It is key to magical manifesting in all areas, especially money (and a lot of money), which is just energy!

However, even though it's simple, it's not always easy.

Boy, do I get it! I know how hard it can be to really get results as we get started. Often, our manifesting doesn't happen consistently, so we have trouble trusting that all this is real. This tends to happen when we don't start out with the necessary self-worth we need to truly embrace this magical way of being. And even if we are open to magic, some of us still have many lessons to work through before seeing consistent results.

It can be especially hard to watch as others proceed at a faster pace. It can also be extremely difficult for people to trust something they cannot see. They have trouble learning to listen to stillness or getting quiet. They've tried meditation but get constantly distracted.

Even after learning a few tricks, they may not know how to bring this way of thinking and being into their professional lives. They feel stupid meditating about a business decision or meditating for positive results in a business meeting.

Others don't like the idea that most of our experiences are created by the energy that we put out and the vibrations we send out every second. This challenges their sensible, traditional, spiritual, and religious beliefs.

If someone is raised hard-core Catholic or had another very religious upbringing, it's hard for them to see the *magic* in spirituality. It's nearly impossible to see magic as *trusting God*. It's difficult to accept the idea that the spirituality that happens from listening to our soul or using our power to manifest, is the exact same spirituality that comes from God. It's even more difficult to believe that God has given us this power and this is on purpose, that He wants us to exercise this creative power, or that He has carefully placed our desires in our hearts to use as part of our internal, God-given GPS system. (I get giddy with goosebumps when I think about this and how all of us can tap into this beautiful and powerful way of being.)

The idea that we create our experiences through our energy and vibrations makes some people feel blame. It feels as if *they* are causing all the bad things to happen in their lives. It's important to understand the difference between accepting responsibility and accepting blame, and I never assign blame to those who've had horrible things happen to them. To take it a step further, I'd add that the terrible things that happen in life are happening *for* us and not *to* us. This slight adjustment is the key to taking back our power.

Lastly, even for those who fundamentally believe and are excited about watching the changes, they sometimes feel that there are not really enough people or power to change the status quo or to make a dent in corporate America and the good ole boys club. You're not alone in your struggle to become a Corporate Hippie. It can take some effort and dedication.

I can only assure you that I'm here to help, and I've already helped many just like you. I've consulted teams to greater gains. Given corporate speeches to help make real and lasting, foundational changes within companies…one person at a time.

The testimonials you may have read in the front of this book are not just a testament to the life changes that these teaching can bring. They are also a testament to the most important life I could have ever possibly changed…

My own.

NOTES

Happiness is your birthright.

Kimberly Adams

Chapter 2

IT WASN'T ALWAYS THIS WAY

I didn't start life as an obvious candidate for a divine leader and manifestor. I was a late bloomer labeled with a low IQ who sought comfort in anything that numbed me out. I was a compulsive overeater and textbook underachiever. I was raised to be plastic and materialistic, valuing looks, clothes, and keeping up with the Joneses. At the same time, I faced sexual abuse from a cousin's step-father.

This man did it in a way that felt good. Can you even imagine the shame and guilt that plagues a young, 13-year-old girl who finds pleasure in being touched by some old, drunk uncle-in-law?

It was humiliating, and I felt so dirty. When I told my mother, I got no protection and no explanation. She just passed it off as a normal, accepted part of being attractive.

My parents divorced, and because I was the oldest, I practically raised my brother and sister. And my mother.

As a young college student, things got even harder. I developed an eating disorder that began damaging family relationships. Worse, it also started disrupting my studies and, ultimately, my ability to graduate college in a timely manner.

In true underachiever form, I flunked out of college. I was forced to work for horrible people, and this led me even further down the path of despair. I knew I needed help. I just didn't know what to do. And every day, it got worse and worse.

But someone was working on a plan, a way to help me…if I would let him.

Dad.

He couldn't stand by, watching helplessly as I slid down this self-destructive path. Being the strong, caring, wonderful man that he is, Dad came up with that desperately needed plan.

He helped me get accepted into an eating disorder program, and even as I was checking in, I felt something shift inside me. I realized that something had to change. I knew that I couldn't accomplish all of my dreams because being 188 lbs. wasn't the true me.

My Inner Guru was telling me that I had more to give to the world and ultimately to myself, and this was the first time I remember feeling the message inside my body. Though I didn't recognize it fully yet, this was my beginning to finding my truth, trusting my intuition, and designing my own destiny. I began my journey to healing.

But I was working for a dentist who paid me crap wages and was cruel and abusive. He made going to work extremely difficult much of the time. I was trapped without a college degree and stuck working for this *Little Shop of Horrors* dentist.

He was awful. And it wasn't just verbal.

He would stab me with instruments while I was working with patients.

He allowed old men in the dental chairs to grope me as we worked on them.

He made me believe that his was a normal working environment. I remember being so upset one time that I called an 800 radio talk show to get advice on how to handle this man.

The worst of it was that I knew I was betraying myself. I knew I was destined for more. Somehow, even back then, I felt in my body and Inner Guru a deep *knowing* that this wasn't my destiny. I knew there was a magical leader inside of me who, if given the chance, could produce big results.

But my self-confidence was still very low.

I wasted the next few years of my life believing that I wasn't worthy of more and that I was going to be stuck in a dead-end job, bending over and working on people's teeth while being groped. It was a very deflating environment, and I hadn't learned how to focus on manifesting magic. I was just literally going from one day to the next.

Then one day, I remember standing in my boss's office. He was pissed at me for something that, looking back, I'm pretty sure was his fault anyway. But instead of taking responsibility, he looked at me and shouted, "If it wasn't for me, you'd be working at Jack in the Box!"

You'd think I would have been pissed at him. Or hurt. Maybe I was, but more importantly, I felt something rise up inside. My soul woke up and knew that was a NO! I felt a literal change inside my body, and I stopped to listen.

It was my Inner Guru, and it told me that this was not going to be my story; there was more for me than a fast-food career. She also told me that there was more for me than a career with a belittling, Jerk-of-a-Boss dentist. My Inner Guru told me that it was time for me to start my path to finding what was truly in store for me.

The only thing left for me to do was to manifest a new opportunity and leave this one.

Within two weeks, synchronicity and divine timing came into play. I was out of there and working at another dentist office, a better one. This new job turned out to be my first Spiritual family at work. And yes, I absolutely manifested it!

I was in a better job environment, my health was continuing to improve, but I was about to be engaged to the wrong guy. Luckily, the people around me cared enough to tell me their concerns. My dad and stepmom offered to pay for me to try a therapy session with a counselor after the eating disorder unit, and I was strong enough to say, *Why not?*

I was strong enough to listen. Trusting my father when he wanted me to go was one of my early turning points because it taught me that I *could* trust.

I met with Donna LeBlanc. In our very first session, she changed my life. She called me on my bullshit. Was I really going to live my life as a dental assistant in Tulsa, Oklahoma, married to the wrong guy (I was engaged at the time)? She started a spark that put me on a different trajectory because I knew I had to call off getting married and moving to Oklahoma. I left there knowing I would not get married, and we continued our deep therapy and healing of my inner child. It was hard work, but I knew that I was worth the effort.

It was time to go back to college and finish. But I had a huge problem. I had a (drumroll please) 0.00 grade point average. To get that GPA expunged from my record so that I could go back to school, I had to show there was a medical reason for it. So, I requested my records from the eating disorder clinic. I took a peek inside the folder and read a comment from a doctor—a psychiatrist to be exact.

Her words leaped off the page at me as I read about my below-average IQ. She wrote that I would never graduate college and basically that I should just have some menial, low paying skilled labor job. I remember thinking that they obviously didn't take into consideration how much being depressed, overweight, and in a hospital impacts one's ability to test well. I also remember thinking that I didn't care what this woman thought. I was getting my college degree. Once again I felt something rise up in my soul saying...knowing...*screaming* that I would graduate college—it was part of my destiny!

Of course, even with this renewed strength and determination, it was hard because neither of my parents had college degrees. So, I didn't have a solid roadmap for how to achieve such a big goal. I just clung to the resolution that to get going on my path of building self-worth and self-confidence, I needed that piece of paper. And I got it.

I worked hard to earn my college degree and continued to practice manifesting. After experiencing manifest after manifest, after watching miracle after miracle, I now have a ton of confidence in my ability to manifest the shit out of life. Over these last twenty-five plus years, I've become a very successful businesswoman, motivational speaker, and author. I started out in my first corporate job earning $7000 a month and have quantum manifested millions of dollars. After being hired by YuMe in 2013, and with the help of my spiritual work family, I grew the company's southwest regions' revenue up from $700K to almost $30MM in just six years. I've also coached teams on methods to help them become more successful.

All in all, I've learned a lot about myself and the world as a result of my earlier challenges. Even after an unsuccessful first marriage, I'm now with my partner for life, Dave, and his wonderful kids Conor, Emilio, and Natalia. These children, along with my first husband's children Taylor and Tyler, have made me what I have coined a *Magical Bonus Mom* because all five children are the best bonuses I could have ever manifested. I get excited when I think about how these spiritual tools can help all five of my bonus kiddos.

I've discovered that I am a powerful creator of magic and that, if I let my body speak to me, my Inner Guru knows all the answers. It's my job to be still and listen. This helped me to finish my college degree, get to a healthy weight, and gain the self-confidence I needed to continue on this magical, spiritual journey.

I overcame my own fears that I wasn't smart enough, and I trusted the Universe (even though I didn't have these terms at the time). I trusted the synchronicity of divine right people being put in my path to help me reach all the desires of my heart.

I also learned that the Universe synchronizes everything for our greatest and highest good. Even when we are questioning or going through those gut-wrenching, dark-night-of-the-soul moments, it is oftentimes a gift.

I couldn't have told you twenty-five years ago that these challenging and sometimes horrible experiences would be pivotal in my discovery of how important it is to believe in magic. I didn't know then that tears are magic drops that can move us toward our manifesting beyond our wildest dreams. I know now this is true, and it can be true for you too!

It's time for the old way of doing things to make way for the new.

OLD: As we've hit on earlier, the old way of defining a hippie is not the way I see it. For some, the word "hippie" brings up a less than favorable image. It can conjure images of radicals, marijuana and Birkenstocks. Many think of Woodstock. Long, stringy hair. Unprofessional. Liberal. Groovy. 60s peace love flowers. Freeloaders who take advantage of the system. They are not looking to be entrepreneurs. They don't contribute to America. They're just bums.

NEW: But I ask, "What's wrong with wanting to have groovy love and peace at work?" What if today's hippie, especially today's Corporate Hippie, brings up a totally different image? Today's Corporate Hippie:

- Uses compassion and intuition to guide them in their business decisions
- Leads from their heart
- Is a lightworker
- Infuses joy, love, and balance in their leadership role
- Tie-dye isn't a requirement, but they might occasionally wear it just for fun!

Any of this sound like you? If so, you may already be well on your way to being a Corporate Hippie! This brings us to another old and antiquated idea that none of this really belongs in the corporate or professional setting.

OLD: In the old way of thinking, none of this love, magic, and intuition stuff belongs in the office and for a number of reasons. One is that they just don't believe in it at all. Another reason is that even if they believe in it, they think of it as a personal belief system. Many see it as a distraction or an unprofessional way to run a business, or worse, unimportant. But what if this stuff is actually profitable?

NEW: Choosing to be a free spirit, and wanting these elements in your life doesn't mean that you have to be opposed to banging it out or starting a business. Being spiritual can also mean wanting to work hard, finding success, and making a lot of money. A whole lot of money.

Would it surprise you to know that more and more of the top companies now encourage meditation as a regular practice? We are starting to see how mixing the corporate with the hippie and using these woo-woo principles are actually helping companies to get ahead. They are leading by example, promoting meditation—*yes!* Even while at work!

Companies like Google, Nike, Yahoo, HBO, and Apple sponsor and lead retreats, meditation classes, mindfulness workshops and courses. They offer designated times for meditation and in-office yoga. Many have quiet rooms, and not just for meditation, but also for prayer and naps.

Google believes that meditation doesn't just help its employees, it also adds to their profits. And I agree.

In the following chapters, we'll dive a little deeper into some key elements and practices. You'll see first-hand just what goes into being a Corporate Hippie and how to use these skills to enhance your professional and personal life.

OLD: And then there's God. Many people think that to be a Corporate Hippie, you can't believe in God. They do not approve of using magic to create our days, nor do they believe in using astrology or practicing yoga. I often find these folks are mostly afraid of losing their traditions. They think that turning inward is taking the place of the Church. They believe that having faith in signs and feelings and trusting in our Inner Guru takes the place of God. But what if it's not like that at all?

NEW: What if having faith in signs and feelings and trusting in our Inner Guru doesn't take the place of God, but rather, it's just an extension of God's brilliance? It's an extension of His ability to delegate. For example, our Inner Guru, our God-given GPS, is a tool that God has given to guide us. God is ultimately the creator of wellness. Some interpret "God's will" as His plan for us. But what if His plan for us is simply our own uncovering of our greatest lives? What if we just let go and allowed it?

And what if we were open to the idea that we all can experience Church anywhere? Even Jesus, on many occasions, questioned the constraints of the establishment over the people. He knows better than any that we can have church anywhere. Together with others or just yourself.

Even sitting out on the grass or driving in your car. I believe that you can create your own Church anywhere.

Most importantly, it is God who has given us so much internal access to improving our lives, finding our paths, and following our dreams. It's all so very possible, and I want everyone to feel and to know this experience. I wish I had known at age twenty that I had access to this. I would be a Gazillionaire by now. I am kind of jelly of all the young people that can tune in early. Part of my journey is introducing these spiritual tools to all of my bonus kiddos whom I deeply love. I get giddy when I think about helping raise enlightened little humans who get to find their answers within through trusting their Inner Guru and having a divine connection with God.

Can you imagine having an unshakeable belief in your worth? That's what is available to you now.

TIP: Every aspect of your life is Spiritual!

When you reassure yourself with positive thoughts and affirmations, you open your body and mind to the highest levels of your spiritual self. One way to tap into your spirituality is hearing your own voice talking to you. Now, don't worry! I'm not suggesting you start having long conversations with yourself. That would make your mom worry. Or your dad. Or your kids. Or your puppy. And no one wants to worry the puppy! She'll start chewing everything up, dig up the yard (or worse—the couch), and hide your shoes.

Instead of risking being committed, try recording yourself speaking ten affirmations, and then play them back in a moment of stillness. It is extremely powerful and healing to hear your own voice giving affirmations!

One of my favorite affirmations is, *I am a powerful Creator!*

But over twenty-five years ago, I had a different favorite affirmation, which led to one of my first big manifesting success stories. It happened after watching Oprah Winfrey's show on manifesting. As she was (and still is) the Queen of Manifesting, I took everything she said to heart.

We (the audience) were instructed to write down a monthly sum that we wanted to earn. It was supposed to be some outrageous amount of money that we almost didn't think could be possible to manifest. Being the devotee that I was, I did it.

I remember writing down, "I'm making over $7,000 per month." Over and over, I wrote it. *I make over $7,000 per month. I make over $7,000 per month. I make over $7,000 per month.* I then affirmed it over and over. I taped it up on my mirror in my bathroom.

Now, I'm warning you, what happens next is in the *you can't make this shit up* category.

Within three months of watching that episode, I landed a sales job at Broadcast.com, where I worked for Mark Cuban (you'll hear more about how that came about in a later chapter), and *Boom!*

Just like magic, just like waving a wand, I was catapulted to that $7000 income level. I went from making roughly $1,100 per month to the next year making $92,000 while hitting $7,600 per month. *I am happy to say that since then, I've never earned less than that ever—COVID notwithstanding! And now, COVID has launched my new entrepreneurial direction and the journey to writing this book, from which the money will continue to flow, flow, flow...*

It's similar to the Jim Carrey story. You know, the one where he writes himself a check for $10 million, and in the memo, he writes, "For acting services rendered." Look how that turned out!

This stuff works. It's real.

As I consider this, I think it's time for me to write a check to myself for my advance as an author and a few more for other motivational speaking and entrepreneurial ideas. While I'm at it, and in the spirit of giving back, I am writing a check for 20% of this new and exciting income. This check is to a charity (either to women or animals or both!). I gotta get to manifesting!

It all starts with those affirmations that bring you to the highest levels of your spiritual self. When you think of the things you want, what might be some of your favorite affirmations?

Write down a list of ten affirmations right now!

NOTES

You yourself, as much as anyone in the entire universe, deserve your own love and affection.

Buddha

Chapter 3

HEART-DRIVEN LEADERSHIP

*I*t's the new millennia. I'm in Mexico (or maybe a spa…?), and my boss calls me. Now, I've never been a fan of bosses invading vacations, but I answer anyway.

"Kim!" his jovial voice puts me at ease. Mostly. But still, I'm waiting for the hammer to drop. Had I screwed up an account? Did we lose someone? Is he calling to fire me?

"Kim," he says, "you close more business when you're on vacation than I've ever seen anyone close!"

I laugh, instantly relieved, and say, "Yeah, because I'm relaxed and having fun. I'm in my flow."

My boss learns an important principle that day. One he'll never forget.

Doing the right things will always come back to you. When you're hiring the right people, when you're leading from your heart, and you're coaching with these new spiritual tools and principles, you are going to get results. You will. The Universe is going to respond to that in a big way. It has to.

Needless to say, this conversation wasn't the last one we had about this, and my vacations were numerous, fun, and profitable for everyone!

******

Heart-driven leadership comes from the top. It must be at the core of every business, every organization, even every relationship dynamic. It means leading with compassion. It's caring about the overall wellbeing of your employees. It's wanting what's best for the people working for you. This is what drives true success in all forms. It creates life-long loyalty and life-changing results. This may sound like the whimsical ideals of a Corporate Hippie, but ethics in business have long been studied.

In the *Graziadio Business Review Journal*, "Love: The Heart of Leadership" by Verl Anderson, Ph.D., Cam Caldwell, Ph.D., and Blair Barfuss, MHR, love stands out as the top leadership ethic to attain. The article suggests that what generates trust is love, not fear. It emphasizes author Steven Covey's strong belief that a leader's most basic and primary responsibility is to share love and give trust while showing, not just talking about, continuous effort and dedication to raising those that follow to their absolute highest potential. I like to call it their "best and highest."

The article also highlights some old ways of thinking. These principles include believing that employees are there for production above all. Businesses should stay just shy of illegal, and do only what you *must* and not what you *should*. It shows that the shift away from such mentalities is critical for continued success in today's businesses. With scholars now studying the science behind showing love in the workplace, they are finding that leaders who develop and share love as an inter-personal quality can push organizations to "achieve greater long-term wealth and add value to the world." Not a bad combination!

Sorry, but the boys club mentality is no longer how profitable companies will get to operate. Things are changing as we speak, and now more than ever it's time to make solid steps towards heart-driven management.

By leading from a place of compassion, joy, and wanting the best for others, we are no longer ego-driven. When you allow the heart to lead your decision-making process, you can drop down into your heart versus your brain. Your heart gives you the clarity that your brain does not. Your brain simply acknowledges and assimilates this clarity. But the heart taps into the Universe, and the Universe gives our hearts access to every answer. Heck, the cosmos is available to us in our hearts! Nothing is held back. But this is not available to us in our brains.

Our logical, rational, reptilian brains only work with facts. The brain can only acknowledge what it sees and knows. Its old-school thinking is driven by ego and fear. We're afraid to make mistakes, and we don't want to look stupid.

In contrast, our hearts give us access to the Universe. Remember, we literally have access to the whole Universe inside our hearts. How can we *not* be successful when we're tapping into this heart energy for our companies? How can we *not* be successful when we are using our heart while we're hiring our team, or operating our businesses? Or when we all work towards a common goal?

How can you *not* be successful when you're allowing and encouraging your teams to tap into their hearts to do whatever they're supposed to be doing? Can you imagine how it would be if you gave your employees this freedom? What ideas would they have? What solutions could they uncover? Especially those in creative roles or sales. Of course, whatever role they're in, how successful will they be when they can bring their full selves to that job in a way where there are not so many parameters and not too much rigidity around them?

Just look at it from your point of view. When your boss or leader is heart-driven and cares deeply for you, you feel it. You feel it, and so will your team. And when team members feel it, you're going to keep them much, much longer than you would if you hire from old paradigms or old models.

In fact, if any of you readers are in Human Resources and want to talk about this, put in a call to me now or just send me a DM @ManifestwithKim because this is *truth… Boom!*

People are becoming less and less willing to work the way they're working now. They're just not going to take it anymore. There's too much crap and there are way too many greedy, self-serving business practices that have been allowed to reign far too long.

Ultimately there will always be those companies and bosses that aren't interested in heart-driven leadership, and it's important to stay away from them. Recognize when someone is going to be so *tunnel vision*, so rigid, or so fear-driven that they can't help but operate in fear and intimidation. A corporation or boss like that isn't going to be a fit for you anyway.

The bigger problem is the loss of profit. What is it going to cost *not* to operate in love? If you're hiring people and then losing them in nine months or two years, you're also losing all the intellectual property, all the time and energy, and all the effort. So, why not make it easy on yourself by offering work conditions that attract the best.

Because at the end of the day, who wouldn't want to work this way? Who wouldn't want to work for a company where the boss actually cares about you and your success? Who wouldn't want a boss that respects all facets of your life, not just what you do for them in the course of eight hours? This brings up another great point.

Nowhere is it written that you have to work 8-5 to get shit done, right? Nowhere is it written that you have to drive an hour to get to work and stay there. COVID-19 has been a bit of a wake-up call in this regard.

If you're empowered and you're operating as an inspired whole, using all these principles, who says you can't get it all done in six hours, or four, or even two sometimes? You get it done and go enjoy the rest of the day with your kids! We go from paying people a tiny pittance so we can own specific (and often way too many) hours of their life, to paying them for the outcome of their efforts, their expertise.

Caring for our employees sometimes means that at some point they may move on and not work for us anymore. I'm okay with that because I'll know that I will have touched their lives in a meaningful way and that they're going to be better off for having had me in their lives.

Some people worry that it's a waste to give them so much freedom, self-improvement, and training only to watch them quit and go do their own thing. Again, I know that I will have given them the best of me. And whether I'm hiring them to work with me forever or I'm hiring them as a stepping stone to their next big adventure, they are valuable, and the journey we've taken is valuable.

Who are we to stomp on someone else's dream? If they want to go start their own business, or if continuing to work for me is not in the cards for them, they move away or whatever, it's all okay. To me, it's about a heart-to-heart connection with our employees and wanting the best and highest for them.

As the saying goes, people are in our life for a reason, a season, or a lifetime. And while obviously none of us want to make mistakes about hiring people, we all do it. But then, is it a mistake? Or is it what's meant to be?

When you're looking for ways to implement heart-driven management, it starts with making small changes. And it starts by taking a personal approach. Start trying to adopt some of the principles of stillness. In this stillness, seek signs.

In other words, carve out a few minutes every day to get still. What's the first thing that comes into your heart when you are still? We can often find a powerful message in that stillness. Try asking for a sign when you're not certain. Ask, *Universe please show me a sign if we are going to close that big deal. Show me a sign if I should hire Susie or Joe?* You get the idea. As you begin doing this more and more, you'll find that you become more in tune with receiving the answers. Now, you don't need to ask to see a frog. However, I do highly recommend that you think of a sign that is unique to you.

To practice stillness, try driving your car in silence. Pay attention to the road, the other cars around you. Notice the sky, the pedestrians on the sidewalk. Is it sunny? Rainy? Give these things you notice no value and no judgment. Try not to react to the traffic and the conditions, simply experience them.

Trying activities even as little as these will begin to awaken and sharpen your intuition.

Also, try bringing in someone like myself or other spiritual manifestors to lead a group meditation. Kick off your calls and meetings with a moment of silence or an uplifting quote, even if they are Zoom meetings. If your team is working from home, hire someone to lead yoga. Plan for future conferences and retreats. Include these practices as part of your wellness program. Many companies, such as Goomi Group, are now offering these to your company in person or via Zoom.

Here's the thing. COVID happened. It's catapulting the need to adjust, or in some cases completely change, the trajectory of how people need to work. Whether your company has 20 employees, 500 employees, or 500,000 plus employees, you could be setting the stage to help your employees to deal with all the uncertainty and anxiety with these spiritual tools.

Here's the other thing. Corporations and even smaller businesses have already become used to bringing in coaching and training for many aspects of career life such as sales training, sexual harassment training, and more.

Therefore, is it really such a stretch to bring in coaches and training for practices that are now proving to increase productivity and bottom line profits? Practices like meditation, stillness, yoga, listening to your intuition, and heart-driven leadership? Let these practical principles join the ranks to become a new corporate paradigm.

TRY THIS for leading with your heart

When life throws uncertainty and ambiguity your way, how do you respond? Can you laugh it off? Or, does it throw you?

This is where the magical power of self-trust comes in handy. Our reptilian brains tend to make us doubt ourselves, even when we know we are right. For thousands of years, this was a good thing because doubt kept our species alive. However, we no longer need doubt to keep us safe or alive. Now, we need trust.

Take a moment right now…put your hands on your heart and be still for one minute.

Ask your heart an important question like one of the following:

- *Which one do I hire?*
- *Is now the time to expand?*
- *Should I ask for a raise?*
- *Will we get this big deal?*
- *Are we on target to achieve our goal?*
- *Are there any changes that would benefit the organization?*

Now, wait for the answer. Your heart knows all the answers and when you learn how to listen, you can change your life in an instant. Of course, feel free to ask other questions about relationships, love, and other impactful decisions in your life. It works!

Listening to your heart is your Superpower.

NOTES

*Listening to your heart
is your superpower.*

Kimberly Adams

Chapter 4

STILLNESS IS WHERE THE MAGIC HAPPENS

*F*or years I've been in a director position at YuMe, and now there's an opportunity to move up to a VP role. This would be a higher leadership role for me, but it would change the whole direction of my team and bring a lot of change and confusion. On the other hand, this offer is coming while I'm going through my break up with Dave, leaving me with plenty of time to pour myself into my work. But I'm not sure if I should take the position.

I need an answer and fast.

So, I get still. Over the next several days, I carve out moments of stillness. Sometimes I spend five minutes in stillness, sometimes ten or twenty. Sometimes even just one minute. I make sure to leave the radio off while I'm driving so that I can have stillness there. I ask for a sign or a message to confirm if I'm truly supposed to take this job of being VP.

I'm listening to Gabbi Bernstein's audiobook, *The Universe Has Your Back*, and I get a clear message as to how I'm going to know. It's for the Universe to show me an owl. So, I ask my guide, my spiritual self, to show me an owl.

Then I say, "No, no, I don't want to see an owl. I want to see a bluebird." Not sure why, but sometimes that's how it goes.

About six hours later, I'm watching a movie, and I get my answer. A very clear message comes to me. On the screen, there's a table with an owl plate on it. Interesting. Okay, well, there's my owl. Ten minutes later in the movie, the entire picture frame is taken over by a bluebird. And can you guess what the characters in the film were talking about?

The bird's leadership qualities!

My spiritual guides and my intuition are obviously showing me, or rather telling me, yes! This is the role to take. The Universe is saying, *Not only are we going to show you the silly, old owl that you didn't want, but we're also going to show you the bluebird so that you will know how much you are loved. How much you can actually trust your Inner Guru.* Yes!

I'm looking at that bird and am now full-on trembling, shaking, crying, and believing that God is so good, and my prayers are real and being answered. Warp speed answered, might I add. The Universe is showing me…me, Kim, how important I really am.

I accept the promotion, and it turns out to be one of my greatest career (and personal) decisions ever. It's great pay, and the best part is that it would eventually allow me to transfer to Orange County, California. Why would I want to move there, you ask?

As you may remember, this all happened when Dave and I were still broken up. And had we been together at that time, I never would have taken this VP role because it would have taken time away from us. I wouldn't have been meditating as much, so I wouldn't have trusted my Inner Guru or my signs.

And that's the whole beauty and irony of it all. By taking the new position, I am able to keep my job with my spiritual family, move to Orange County, where Dave lives, and remain gainfully employed! Yay, Me!

Really, my friend, this is the kind of crazy shit you can't make up!

You can't make up the synchronicity of these kinds of events, even seemingly disappointing or challenging events like someone not showing up to an interview (or breaking up with the love of your life). You just have to trust the flow of everything. But when you start to force it, you are doing a disservice to yourself, to the other team members, to the company.

******

Stillness is literally life-changing. That feathery sign came to me only *after* I had started regularly practicing stillness in meditation, and it turned out to be exactly right. I haven't been the same since.

This evidence changed me on a cellular level. I felt completely and totally connected to my Soul. While some people think that meditation is just for monks in Tibet, or believe they have to be silent for an hour to get benefits, this is not the case. You can experience stillness before you take your feet out of your bed. It all comes down to making stillness a practice and starting where you can, even if it's for just 1 minute.

We all can agree that anything worth having is worth developing some sort of practice to make it happen, whether it's daily or every other day or whatever suits your style best. There has to be some sort of conscious thought of being still.

And as we can see, with big businesses like Google and General Mills incorporating mindfulness training, this practice is not about fluffy unicorns in tie-dye saddles. It's about the science of the brain and its reaction to meditation and stillness. Take the amygdala section of our brain, for example. Yes, we're using some big words here. While I believe in this magic without the need for scientific proof, it's always interesting to see how these principles are scientifically explained, especially for those who feel a little skeptical!

Our amygdalae (we each have two) are located in the temporal lobes of our brain near our hippocampus. They are responsible for or are associated with feeling certain emotions such as fear and anxiety, some behaviors like aggression, and even motivation or—on the other side of the spectrum—psychiatric disorders.

According to Bruno Dubuc, this area of the brain fires survival instincts and modulates all of our reactions to events. That's what has allow our species to survive.

The *Harvard Gazette's* article, "When science meets mindfulness" shares the work of Harvard Medical School radiology instructor, Gaëlle

Desbordes. Desbordes' work reveals MRI scans of the amygdalae in our brains that are affected by sustained weeks of meditation, and not just when meditating, but also after. The scans suggest that meditation helps the amygdalae to function better.

Still, we might ask, how is this helpful at work?

In the *US National Library of Medicine National Institutes of Health* 2019 Journal publication, "Mindfulness meditation for workplace wellness: An evidence map," by Lara G. Hilton, Nell J. Marshall, Aneesa Motala, et al, the authors reference the new the rise of written evidence among business and phycological peers alike linking mindfulness to improving function in the workplace.

The study documents the potential benefits of meditative work to relieve pain, anxiety, perceived stress, and more.

Imagine a workplace that focuses on lowering stress. How productive could your team grow in the absence of anxiety, depression, pain, or chronic illness? How much faster can you meet your career goals when your body and mind begin working for you, rather than you continuing to struggle to make it from one meeting to the next?

What are the far-reaching effects of stillness in our careers? When Jack Canfield decided to make his first hundred thousand dollars, he had to develop the belief it could be done and set up the intention. Back then, a hundred thousand dollars was an exorbitant amount of money. Jack chose this amount as a test because he could see no possible way to earn it without using the power of intention—especially with an earned annual income of only $8,000.

With the help of his mentor, W. Clement Stone, he set the intention. He continually got still and visualized his new $100,000 lifestyle, and every time he got an *idea,* Jack put it to the test by acting on the idea. He was surprised at how the Universe worked to bring together the people and events that would help to manifest the income.

Jack ended up selling his self-published book, *Chicken Soup for the Soul,* from an interview published in *The National Enquirer.* He made $92,327 that year, just shy of his goal, but they weren't disappointed! Then he asked his mentor if this would work for a million.

It's easy to imagine his smile when Jack received the million-dollar check on the advance for the first traditional publication of his book.

Whether you own your own business or work for someone else, you can use the powers of stillness and intention to bring in extra income, the right connections, or even the perfect circumstances to manifest your intentions. No goal is too big, no amount is too high, and no dream is undeserving when it's truly coming from your heart and not your ego. Our desires are a dream away, as my favorite band, Coldplay, tells us (a bit more eloquently, I admit).

You are precious and divine. By all rights, you deserve the best life. You are worthy of a business that is booming or a job that is a financial and an emotional blessing. It is in growing still and allowing that your intentions can finally have the room to develop and come to pass.

TRY THIS for mastering stillness and setting intentions

Set intentions that actually manifest such as being silent in the car or choosing self-care as a priority. Start with intentions that you know that you can accomplish. Get very still. Go within, and search your heart for your intentions.

- What's your dream job? Where are you? At a desk, your own home, traveling?
- What are your year-end (or quarterly) goals? Visualize yourself and what it feels like getting that enormous check.
- Do you have a long-term dream, plan, or goal that seems unattainable but that you really want? Write it down. Meditate, be still, and be consistent with your practices.

Get very clear on a few very specific intentions. Write down a few easy intentions, a few more challenging intentions, and a few bigger, life changing intentions. Like Jack Canfield, you can prove to yourself that it could only have been achieved through the powers of intention and stillness.

One very powerful addition to this practice that I've learned is that once you write your intentions, desires, and dreams, be sure to leave room for more. Say, "Please bring me these desires of my heart or something better." Sometimes God has in mind something more expansive, beyond our wildest dreams, or something more than we could've ever imagined.

TIPS

Use these six intention-setting questions to help you manifest anything you want (remember to find some stillness before you ask these questions).

1. Why are you choosing this intention? There are no right or wrong answers, and it may take some time to find a reason that resonates with you.

2. How will this intention make you feel? If your intentions don't move you, excite you, or thrill you in some way, I hate to break it to you...but you might have a hard time manifesting them. Our feelings are very attached to our higher selves. When we're feeling bad about something, or univested, it's best to examine the intention and perhaps even swap it out for one that creates a strong, positive reaction.

3. How can you anchor the intention to your daily life? Anchors allow you to leave little hints to yourself about your intentions. For example, you can set a daily notification on your phone with a positive affirmation of your intention. You can stick a Post-it with your affirmation to your steering wheel or bathroom mirror. Try putting an object that symbolizes the intention in your pocket. These reminders keep you *anchored* to your intentions by reminding you of them throughout your busy day. Put anchors in as many places as you can to remind you that your intentions are really happening for you.

4. Are you ready to take action? The Universe can only do so much. You must be willing to set the path through the Universe

for the manifestation to guide itself. There is a delicate balance between allowing and acting. You must allow the Universe to guide you while at the same time, be prepared to act on the guidance and signs of the Universe so that the intention can manifest.

5. Do you believe this intention will manifest? Can you visualize it? This is critically important because the power of belief drives and manifests your intentions. Belief can allow you to achieve your intention in record time and often with minimal effort. However, even when we do believe, sometimes it still does take a lot of time or more effort. How much more difficult is it to manifest your intention without belief?

6. How long are you willing to wait for it? There are times when it seems to take forever. The Universe does not work on our schedule, so we must be patient and trust in divine timing. We must surrender.

Remember to keep in mind that while stillness and meditation are a must, it's important to follow up with action. More importantly, base your action on what your Inner Guru is telling you, whether as a result of spending time in stillness or listening to your gut feeling.

Now, it's time to align your thoughts with your actions. Start *doing* rather than just *thinking! Let's make some MAGIC!*

Remember:
Intention + Action = Magic

NOTES

Intentions are a business woman's magic spell.

Kimberly Adams

Chapter 5

INNER GURU (YOU GOTTA LISTEN)

*I*t's around 1995. I'm on my second try at getting my college degree, and I've discovered chat rooms. *Back in the day, a chat room was called an Internet Relay Chat.* I'm obsessed with finding out everything about them. It's fun meeting people online, and I guess you could say I'm becoming quite the pioneer of online dating.

I'm also hungry for information, so when this new Internet chat café opens up in Dallas, I'm first in line to check it out. I'll never forget rolling in on my rollerblades one day and striking up a fascinating conversation about chatrooms with Dave Mathews, the Gadget Guy (not to be confused with the Dave Matthews Band, lol).

Dave turns out to be a wealth of information, and in minutes I'm already learning and understanding more about this thing called the World Wide Web.

We exchange numbers, and within twenty-four hours, Dave calls me and asks if I want to be on the groundbreaking TV, radio, and Internet show called *Net Talk Live!* He warns me that I have to meet with the star of the show and executive producer. I should be nervous, but something inside knows better. I'm literally smiling from ear to ear.

Truth be told, I've always imagined and dreamed of being famous. I want to be on this show so much, and I pray with focused attention on manifesting this desire.

When I meet the executive producer and Jovan the star, I already know it's done. My Inner Guru knows the moment I meet them that I'm going to be the first "Chatchick" on *Net Talk Live!*

I'm going to be Chatchick, Kim Adams.

Now, looking back, I can say that any job or opportunity that I ever went for and really wanted, I actually got. My inner knowing and deep sense of trust alongside my innate alignment to my purpose were already working even while I was a baby seeker.

The plot thickens because little do I know that as I embark on this career path, the ground is being laid for an even bigger plan.

A couple of years later, it's 1998. I'm sitting in Mark Cuban's office, hoping to get hired at Broadcast.com (this is before it goes public, and Mark becomes a billionaire). Charles Cooper, Stan Woodard, and a few other executives are all in the room looking at me skeptically.

I've taken the personality test, and Stan tells me my score. It isn't good. In fact, my score's so bad that no one except Stan wants to hire me. I figure I'm toast, but Stan recognizes me as Chatchick, Kim Adams, from *Net Talk Live!*

While this job is very different from chatting about chatrooms and the Internet, Stan trusts that there is something, something he can't put his finger on. He trusts me and decides to give me a shot. His faith in me makes me want to work hard for him. He's taking a chance on me, so I have to prove him right (spoiler alert, he hires me again later, so I guess I do).

My new job has me going out and selling video services to companies that are streaming audio services. IBM is having a product launch in New York and broadcasting internally to five hundred people. Our service is a total cost savings for them because instead of having to fly those people out, they can just go to a URL and watch the presentation complete with PowerPoint. Yup, you guessed it. I'm giving webinars when people don't even know what a webinar is.

I'm also basically killing it, and I get my first commission check. It's $8K! My entire earnings the year before had been less than $15K. *Boom!*

Stan trusting his gut with me is an example of listening to your Inner Guru. He had no evidence that I would make a good employee, let alone a great one. However, his decision to trust brought the company a salesperson whose very first commission check was $8,000. His decision brought the company a go-getter who went on to hit every single sales goal, every single quarter after every single quarter, and who became the company's VIP Salesperson year after year. His decision to trust brought the company a salesperson who made them a whole heck of a lot more than that $8000 commission. His decision to trust his Inner Guru clearly turned out to be a good one, and I would not be where I am today without this pivotal decision from Stan. To this day, I am still so grateful.

It goes to show that we can't put someone in a box just because their scores don't match what we're looking for or because they don't fit our perfect picture. It shows that we really have to listen to and trust our intuition.

Had Stan *not* listened to his Inner Guru, he never would have hired me. I never would have made that company a shitton of money or made enough sell off my division of the company, and Stan and I never would have worked together later to make another shitton of money. It shows that, *yes!* This magic shit does work!

******

We already know the answers. In Terri Williams' article, "Instincts in business: Knowing when to trust your 'gut,'" which appeared in *The Economist*, he talks about the concept of using the *whole body* to help us make the best decisions. He quotes Rick Snyder, author of *Decisive Intuition: Use Your Gut Instincts to Make Smart Business Decisions*, who believes that we are getting signals all day long and clues that can help us make decisions. Snyder emphasizes our need to stay receptive to these signs rather than only trusting our thoughts or rationale because signs give us all the information we need to make the best decisions.

Williams' article also emphasizes the need to discern bad instincts from good intuition. Since I don't believe we have bad instincts, I interpret this to mean that we must differentiate our unreliable reactions from our instincts or intuition.

This reminds me of a date I went on with a guy a long, long time ago. My friends and family had been rooting for us to go out, and so they set us up. Because everyone thought that we would make such a good match, I was pretty excited.

We were at the restaurant, and it was going pretty well. The food was great, the chatting was nice, the atmosphere was perfect. Until he said *something* (to this day, I can't remember what). I caught a look in his eye that I couldn't quite describe, and every hair on the back of my head prickled and stood on end.

I immediately paid attention to the really strong physical reaction my body was giving me, the signs. I felt nervous and my stomach tightened. I knew I had to get out of there, and I left and never saw him again. Nor did I ever really think about him again.

Until after a few years went by, when this guy ended up taking the life of some poor woman.

Had I not listened to my body and the signs it was giving me, that woman may well have been me. My body warned me that night. It protected me. And I listened.

When we're new at listening to our Inner Guru, there can be a learning curve, so it's important to note when we react strongly to something. Luckily for me, it wasn't that I reacted to this guy based on any preconceived notions, past hurtful experiences, fears, or biases, but rather, I listened. Luckily.

Sometimes in the beginning, we tend to respond to our innate needs or expectations instead of what's really happening, so it's important to be certain. We don't want to run from every date thinking the guy's dangerous. But we certainly don't want to ignore when our instincts tune in to the signals.

Our neuroreceptors (present in most of our cells) are constantly receiving and processing the clues around us that we're not often able to see. It's our job to learn to discern the messages accurately. As you practice listening to your instincts and intuition, you'll find that it becomes quite easy to identify the differences between unreliable reactions and instincts.

Trusting your Inner Guru means trusting your intuition, your God-given GPS system. It's using the Universe as a driving guidance and divine force for making business decisions…and all decisions, really. Have you ever made a wrong turn while driving? You either got totally lost or somehow managed to get back on the road. It may come as a surprise to discover that we also have our own inner guidance system!

Our Inner Guru is our GPS system, our intuition, and it is quick to reroute us back on track if we trust it. It's an extremely powerful tool, so if we take the time to understand how it operates, we can actually get where we are going a lot faster. Being able to distinguish our body's *yeses* from our *nos*, reduces many stresses in our lives. Trusting our intuition is a game-changer because it can stop us from taking the wrong job, hiring the wrong person, or dating the wrong dude! It's never too late to change direction.

For every question, there is an answer. For every problem, a solution. Do you know what the crazy thing is?

We already know everything we need to know. This is so important because our God-given GPS system knows what to do in every given situation. For example, when you get a flash that something is not right, believe it. By trusting your gut and body, you can know how to respond or engage. You can also know when and how to initiate.

With business decisions, driving a car, or anything, your body intuitively is that inner GPS System. Your body knows what it needs. It instinctively knows whether you need Advil or Tylenol. Try holding each, and notice if your body moves towards it or away from it. Try comparing broccoli to a piece of pizza. This is how smart our bodies are.

Use your body signs with business practices, with clients, with who you're going to hire. To me, it comes down to asking a few simple questions. How do you want to be guided when making these very large decisions? How do you want to be guided into hiring people who are ultimately going to be part of your team? How do you want to be guided when choosing who will be major players in your life?

If someone doesn't have all the requirements necessary for the role you're hiring, but you know that this person is going to be a Rockstar, or you intuitively know that this person is going to be the person who changes the game for you, do you dismiss them because not all their skills are showing up on paper?

Listening to our Inner Guru's in our careers can help us make the best decisions. It can also open doors to more success than we ever thought possible. In my corporate career, my boss and my team always gave me the freedom and autonomy to make important decisions without question.

I trust my gut. I follow my instincts. I seek the highest and best, sit in stillness, and look for signs. And my decisions are always spot on. In other jobs where people would try to direct me, it didn't always work out all that well because those companies could never inspire or receive my full potential.

Yes, it's good to listen to our Inner Guru, our intuition or instincts, our God-given GPS system. It's also good to seek direction from our Angels, our guides and spirit guides. However, the transformation can only happen when we take this a step further and embrace that these *instincts* or *guides* are really extensions of our inner consciousness. The ultimate truth is, we already know everything that we need to know. Truth and intuitive knowledge are part of our makeup.

I believe that before our souls even came to exist in human form, we made contracts. We knew how things worked and made these contracts long before we came to the planet. Our soul knows what to do. It's our ongoing job to be still and listen.

As the saying goes, *"We are not physical beings having a spiritual experience; we are spiritual beings having a physical experience."*

And whether this phrase was coined by Pierre Teilhard de Chardin, Georges Gurdjieff, or Wayne W. Dyer, the sentiment remains: The power of divinity is at our disposal, for we are not born of dust alone.

We are spirit. We are divine. We are the past, the present, and the future. All questions are born twins to their answers.

Only, we often find that we've forgotten those answers. We grow up experiencing human realities in this world. We often spend so much time worrying about what other people think and expect from us. We go through our daily routines, drink wine, eat, and try to find connection and happiness. Always trying to figure out if we're doing the right thing. When it all boils down to us having always known, right from the start.

How can I be so sure? Remember back to when you were a child. When you were three, four, five and you saw or felt that something was scary or seemed off. You *knew* it, accepted it.

Maybe you sensed an energy current or had a feeling that you knew what was going to happen before it did. You might have had an imaginary friend that was a guide or a spirit that was here to assist you with your life. I can only imagine if I'd been able to tap into the magic when I was a child.

We all know who we are when we're four, and then we spend the rest of our lives losing it, along with the joy we were born to experience. This is the result of living lives with those fears, biases, and life experiences to which Williams referred in his article. All those experiences seep the joy and trust out, one event at a time.

It's time to remember that there is a joy to being alive. There is a joy to being able to live a good life, having beautiful and meaningful relationships, and at the same time, working for a company or for yourself where you're in charge of your destiny.

When you trust your Inner Guru, you don't need to work harder to find more answers. You don't need to try. You don't need books (though, they *are* extremely helpful). You don't need to talk to somebody. If you just get alone with your mind, get aligned with the Universe, and ask a question, you will get the answer. It's just about learning to trust what you're hearing. It's also learning to trust the answers even when they seem to go against what you're thinking that you want.

And this brings us to an important point. We must learn to trust another sign that, for many, doesn't feel like a sign, but rather, it feels like a form of rejection. This sign is *silence*.

Sometimes, the answer is no. Other times the answer is... *crickets*, and you don't get an answer. It often comes down to what question you're asking, or it's the way that you are phrasing the question because subtleties can make a huge difference. It's like the difference between asking, "May I?" vs. "Can I?" For example, you can ask if it's okay to eat hamburgers and chocolate every day. And the answer is, *sure*. But the reality is, what does that do to your body?

TRY THIS to hone listening to your Inner Guru

To implement this in your career, always ask the Universe for the best and highest for all people involved in any situation.

Say you're hiring. Before each interview, stop and ask for what's best for both the applicant and your company. Then listen to your Inner Guru. Let your instincts give you guidance.

Sometimes this will mean that you *don't* hire the person who's the apparent best fit (not that this means that you won't work together later). You might find yourself taking a chance on a seemingly unqualified candidate. Sometimes, connections are all about timing.

Also, signs are information, so be sure to pay attention to them. Back to our hiring example, suppose a confirmed appointment ends up not showing up and not even calling. Maybe they got into a car accident. Maybe their kid got sick, or they got sick or took a wrong turn. Whatever reason, to live your best and highest life, it's your job to trust that this is exactly how it's meant to be.

It's this whole idea of rejection being protection. Like when you have a first date that you're so excited about, but then they flake, and you still give them a second chance. You go out with them, but it turns out to be a disaster.

When you allow flow instead of force, when you trust that all things happen for both of your best, everything ends up better for both of you. Again, it all comes down to the idea that you are being protected, and this person may not the right one for you, or the timing may not be the right timing. The more you trust the process, the more everything will end up better than you ever dreamed possible.

Use this process for deciding who to partner with, vendors, clients, you name it! Trust is always about accepting the gifts, and what might look like a no or a no-win situation will always turn out to be for your best and highest.

TIPS

Remember that meditation and trust will enhance your dream state.

- Practice meditation. Sit silently and still with your thoughts, and focus on your Inner Guru that is guiding you every day. This has been a truly life-changing piece of my journey, and it's my wish for everyone to experience the benefits and beauty of a regular practice of stillness.

- Let go of perfection. Thoughts come and go, and most people worry about that. Don't! There is no perfection in meditation. It's letting go of expectations while meditating that raises vibrations, not worrying about if you're doing it right. Remember, if you are doing it at all, you're doing it right.

- Trust your Inner Guru. Trust your inner self and your inner knowing. Your soul knows all the answers! Understanding this is a huge step for anyone that's on a spiritual path. It's absolutely paramount to rest in this knowledge. Once we embrace this one principle, every challenge or obstacle becomes less threatening. When we know that the answers lie within, it eliminates the endless search for solutions.

NOTES

*A problem cannot be
solved by the same level
of consciousness that
created it.*

Albert Einstein

Chapter 6

SPIRITUAL WORK FAMILIES

I'm sitting at my desk when Pat, the office manager, walks up. She's handing me papers to go through. I'm brand new, having just quit the horribly mean dentist. I'm working in a new dental office. It is so, so much different. I'm treated with respect, and I feel like a team member rather than someone to be exploited. It's a breath of fresh air.

"Have you accepted Jesus in your heart?" Pat asks me out of the blue.

I'm surprised but not so much by the question as I am by what comes after. For the next several weeks, I'm a bit on edge, holding my breath, waiting for the constant comments, the preaching, the judgment. I'm waiting for Pat or Dr. McDougal to start a full-on campaign to save my soul.

It never happens. Instead, all I get is unconditional love and respect. I feel cared about as a person, as an individual, separate from the business of making money.

I'm encouraged to explore my spirituality and to practice seeking but without the strings normally attached by religion. My new office family never tries to force any opinions or agendas on me. They simply perform this beautiful act of caring about me on a higher and deeper level at work. And I'm just so surprised, and I can breathe easy. It's my first exposure to being and feeling like an important and valuable part of a spiritual work family.

This experience is the catalyst for me years later when I'm heading the sales team for YuMe. Ann Piper is my boss during this time, and she one hundred percent allows me to run my team the way I choose. She gives me full autonomy, and I know from the offset that I want our team members to feel the same way my first spiritual work family made me feel.

I choose to lead with my heart, with my intuition, and with compassion. But not just lead, I also share. I coach my team on the principles in this book, such as listening to our Inner Gurus and practicing self-care.

I'm the boss affectionately known as Mama Bear who ends team calls with "Love You!" I'm building a Corporate Hippie style, non-traditional, kick-ass sales team, and I'm doing it with love and joy. I'm sharing the process of being open, showing that I'm the same at work as I am in life. I'm not one person wearing many hats, not one way at work and a different way in life. I am the same, wherever I am. This is me, and this is it.

Since many sellers are Type A personalities and very driven, it quickly becomes my number one goal to be a coach to them and make them successful. This is because being in sales at any level often comes with destructive or sometimes debilitating stressors around performance. Everyone is worried about hitting their numbers. They are concerned with increasing their quota and growing in the company and in wealth. They have to learn to handle those inevitable times when we are going to lose a client, when competitors steal business, or when all the things that can go wrong do go wrong. I don't want my team to feel this stress…

Being that I'm particularly focused on building my spiritual family team here at YuMe, I spend a lot of time reflecting on how much I personally used to stress myself out about hitting those numbers. I am becoming an active seeker of any and all things spiritual, things that will enhance the magic in my life. Instead of allowing stress and force to set in, I encourage them to feel the flow of money coming them. Our whole team does begin to feel that flow as I begin to impart to them the power of my many manifesting tools.

I share the practices and ideas that I've intuitively been using to achieve my best life, such as giving up worrying because that does not drive sales. I show them that being too busy or ambitious to take care of yourself won't bring more sales—that, in fact, it can hurt sales even though it wouldn't seem so. As I discover more ways of not stressing about my job and letting it flow…letting the money flow to me, so does my team.

We use vision boards, journals, and affirmations. We use crystals and wear matching crystal bracelets to bring money magic, better communication, and sharper team skills. I'm always asking, "Are you wearing your crystals?"

We go on yoga trips, spa trips, and it becomes so ingrained that it's a belief on the cellular level. I tell them, "It's in you. That's how you operate."

A tangible example is when a team member is worried about how a client is going to respond to some difficulty or challenge. They may be angry, rude, or even take away their business. When other bosses will fly into panic mode and buzz in circles trying to fix the situation, I encourage my team to use a very effective visualization tool for client conflict.

I tell them, "Before you jump on a call and risk knee-jerk reactions on all sides, stop. Get quiet, and have a quick conversation in your mind to set the stage for the conversation to go smoothly. Say to the Universe (as though you are talking to the client), 'I know we had a difficult situation with the campaign, I know we are going to get through this, thank you for sticking with the program you signed up for.'"

This is exactly how shifts happen…this is what it feels like to create a spiritual family at work. It doesn't mean that it will always work to exorcise all negative response to the situation, but it often does help at least to some degree. Personally, I have seen very difficult business situations change when using this tool.

As a whole, our team's efforts to practice these new principles help us to begin giving up worrying. We learn to allow the Universe to do what it's going to do. And as things begin to flow (our team is #1), we discover that we can indeed trust that the best and highest will come to us when we believe and put into practice certain principles.

When we need a client to sign a contract, they do. When we need money, out of the blue we get it. When we can't fathom hitting our huge sales numbers (especially at the beginning), we meditate, focus on positivity and self-care, and we hit our numbers every year for eight years.

You can't make this shit up!

And our bank accounts don't lie. This whole time, it's raining commission checks.

The years pass, and it's towards the end of my time working with the team. We're dealing with a difficult client situation that I can't seem to solve. I'm feeling unusually tense until Lynsey, who has always been the most skeptical of my methods, says, "Relax, Mama Bear. Mercury is in retrograde,"

I relax instantly, and I know that I can leave here a happy woman. Even Lynsey understands that the forces of the planet aren't in flow for this deal, so we end up not forcing it. And we end up getting something better. As always, it all works out for our team's best and highest.

I write a poem for my team of Diva Badass Ladies to commemorate our time together at YuMe:

> *We are the YuMe girls, yes we are! We've sold*
> *CTV near and far.*
> *Although our journey has come to an end, we*
> *still have each other to call Dear Friends!*
> *I have no words to describe*
> *The love and joy I've felt working beside the*
> *most beautiful ladies—especially on the inside.*
> *Mama Bear is finally ready to let go*
> *And watch her spiritual Badasses grow, grow, grow!*
> *Let's toast to our Angels, Crystals and Guides.*
> *Thank you, Dear Lord, for the*
> *EXTRAORDINARY ride.......*

******

Spiritual work families are the result of truly transformational leadership. We build them by being intentional in our businesses and intentional in how and who we hire. We always want the best and highest for the business as well as for our employees no matter our company's size. We use spiritual practices to create and manifest magic in business (and in life). We integrate the home and the workplace.

"Of course there's separation," one might say at first glance, even me.

But *should* there be separation? Shouldn't we be thinking of the betterment of the people we work with, who we spend more time with than our families? Shouldn't we be wanting the best and the highest for them as well as ourselves? Shouldn't we actively care when there's a sickness in their family? Shouldn't we want balance in this person's life?

It starts with assuming leadership around the whole person, not just an *employee* that you're seeing at the office. Think of the amount of work and the kind of work they do for you. Consider the loyalty you'll get from operating in a way that's led from your heart, that's heart-driven. Know that wanting the best and highest for them as well as yourself actually keeps them working for you and more loyal to you while allowing you to continue to prosper.

And it's not always about the money. How many talented people take positions despite the pay because they love the cause? How many companies, even during COVID, are realizing they need to pay more. They see the big picture that it's about hiring the right people, paying them well, trusting their teams, and knowing that together, all are aspiring to the same high goals.

Spiritual work families represent an evolved way of working in this new world that we're in. It's a world where we are learning that we have to trust these people more, especially as we're letting them into our lives and into our homes with Zoom. It's a world filled with the energy of positivity, of joy, of love, of trusting that everyone is doing their best and their highest together. As we touched on earlier, this is becoming the only way businesses are going to succeed any longer.

Let's break the status quo here by challenging why so many bosses choose not to run their businesses in this new, heart-led way, and so much of this really comes down to one thing.

It's male-led, corporate America. This good ole boys club with its paradigm of going off to play golf together, drink beer together, among other things, and it's not just seen in America. This is just how so much of the world works. We've got this male-dominated system, this checks and balances type of leadership that no longer applies to how things really get done in the workplace or even the world. And if we're being honest here, those balances really don't balance the needs of most hard-working folks like yourself and your friends and family. Those balances tend to lean toward the pocketbooks of these bosses.

And not just the pocketbooks. The balance of sex and power must also be addressed. Numerous women and men have been impacted by sexual harassment while at work. Many are either victims or witnesses to this crime every day. This can no longer continue, and it's time for all of us to take a stand.

If you see something, say something. If someone confides in you, please encourage them to report the incident to Human Resources. Our silence allows this abhorrent behavior to be so pervasive and prevalent.

Be brave!

And for those perpetrators out there, Karma is a bitch, as they say, and it will always catch up.

Unfortunately, I know firsthand what it's like to experience this. It's a painful part of my story that has caused much suffering. I've had to do a lot of inner work to heal, and my heart goes out to everyone who has also suffered or experienced this in a personal or work setting.

I've overcome, and I've thrived because of the work I've put into discovering and honing my spiritual tools. These tools include journaling, meditating, and praying. My experience changed the way I want to work and who I choose to work for, which is why now I work for myself.

Mine and the experiences of others who've also faced sexual harassment are part of why building spiritual families at work is a key element to the movement of foundational change in corporate America.

I'm not just a *survivor* because of my experiences of sexual abuse. In spite of them, I am a *thriver!* And so are you. Together, we can eradicate this poison. We can start or join spiritual family workplaces. We can make a difference for our daughters and sons as they prepare to enter the workforce.

Now, is the time for a change—a woman's touch. In this new Age of Aquarius, we're no longer going to get things done by force. Now, we must have fluidity, flow, trust, intuition, meditation, stillness, and energy to move forward. It's time to take a look at how women affect the economy. No, I'm not referring to how much she's spending. I'm referring to how much women bring to the table. Let's face it. Women just work differently than men, and we've got a lot to add to the business world.

S&P Global is a leading market intelligence firm that collects, analyzes, and presents fully researched data, analytics, and commentary. Top companies turn to S&P for the information they need to make critical decisions that drive profits. Having been around for over 150 years, it's safe to conclude the reliability of the information gleaned and shared by this company.

According to S&P, women-led corporations are more profitable than those led by men. This is seen in the S&P editorial, *When Women Lead, Firms Win,* written by Daniel J. Sandberg, Ph.D. Mr. Sandberg describes the results that women CEOs experience after only 2 years on the job. He shares studies that show that these women see a 20% increase in stock price momentum. He also points out that women CFOs raise stock returns 8% and increase profitability by 6%. Again, this is just in the first two years!

I feel the shift now, and as 2020 gives way to new beginnings, I'm staking my claim that as companies begin to acknowledge the power behind these women-led companies, they will also begin to book more and more meditation and intuitive coaches. Who can afford to not take action with those types of astounding numbers?

The economic and statistical significance of these results are not lost on Sandberg, and his research denounces the still popular opinion of padding the top of the corporate ladder with *token* female executives— the business equivalent of *trophy wives*—rather than actually choosing and using women based on the value we bring to the table. The research supports the need for and the profitability of higher gender diversity not only in leadership positions, but also in the board room. The data shows that increased gender diversity amongst board members adds up to bigger profits than that of organizations with boards including fewer (or no) women.

Part of the reason for this phenomenon, according to Sandberg, is that women are held to higher standards, and therefore must rise to meet and exceed those standards. He goes so far as to write, "Overall, the attributes that correlate with success among male executives were found more often in female executives."

Another reason is that women operate differently. We believe differently. We are able to see the whole picture and different facets of situations.

So, wouldn't this be the time for corporate America to be putting more of an emphasis on women leaders in their companies? Why not use the principles that women inherently and innately have?

In *Forbes'* Senior Contributor, William Arruda's article, "6 Ways COVID-19 Will Change The Workplace Forever," we see that the approach of creating spiritual work families isn't just a woo-woo fantasy. It is, indeed, becoming the norm.

He suggests that flexibility is at the heart of how companies will have to adjust in the post-COVID-19 era. With a Gallup survey indicating that 54% of workers would accept another position that offered remote work, it's no surprise that the pandemic has solidified the need to incorporate this into any business model.

Arruda also predicts that e-learning will become the norm. I agree and would add that e-learning must include personal growth and self-improvement.

TRY THIS for creating a Spiritual Work Family

Remember to always wish for the highest and the best for your employees and yourself. Communicate regularly to make sure that their needs are being met and that they are maintaining work balance. Take the advice of Lewis Howes's article, "5 Secrets to Building a Business - - With Heart," published in *Entrepreneur*:

1. Don't just set your business up to stay barely legal. Create a culture of caring, and take it a step further. Find ways to make your spiritual work family's lives better. Pay them well, inspire them at work, do great good.

2. Care for others because your ultimate success lies in their success. If you truly care about building a business and brand that can stand the current temperature of today's new work ethics, you have to care about your team. Know when they're tired or stressed. Plan excursions and retreats. Demonstrate your goodwill by going out of your way to make sure their needs are taken care of.

3. Let love be your bottom line. It all comes down to love, but it's important to distinguish love as an action, a verb, not just a noun or a desired state. Love is doing for others. Love is demonstrating through actions that you care. Love is allowing your ego to die to selflessness. It's putting your team first. Love is the greatest power that you can infuse into your business, and it's the strongest attracter of all good things.

TIPS on helping your team create their own magic

- Remind them and have them remind themselves every day that they absolutely, unequivocally deserve everything they want.
- Help them to know that the Universe is always listening.
- Encourage them to create vision boards or write in a journal
- Hire an Intuitive Coach

- Encourage them to seek all of the magic available to raise their vibrations and attract the desires of their hearts.
- Ask yourself, "Do I trust and believe this intention can manifest?"

Remember that if you can dream it, you can become it, and remind your team of this fact.

NOTES

Stillness is where the magical shit happens.

Kimberly Adams

Chapter 7

SELF-CARE AND BALANCE

*S*ix weeks until I say, "I do," and I'm on a walk with my sister and stepmom. Six weeks doesn't seem like enough time to get everything done. I feel so stressed, and I'm hoping this walk will help to refresh me.

The air is brisk and refreshing. My sister and stepmom are encouraging me, telling me that I'll be able to get it all done. Of course, they are right. As we stroll along, I feel the anxiety slowly fade.

I get back home and the calm quickly dissipates as my fiancé throws himself into the biggest fit. He's furious that I took time to go out for a walk. I'm watching him as if in a dream and for a moment, I'm in total shock that I'm being yelled at for taking care of myself. He's calling me a bitch. He's calling me the C-word.

The next day, I'm watching Oprah (yes, it's a habit that I adore). She has a guest on that's saying to run away if a man ever calls you these names.

Luckily, I listen. I don't ignore this huge warning flag, and I break it off. I've come to recognize my value, and my worth has been a transformative piece to self-care and ultimately self-love. I've determined to only be around people and friends, work environments, and relationships that support me on my mission to take care of myself.

******

Self-care is not limited to our personal lives and it's imperative to any success. Sure, we all want to look good, make money, and be successful. However, being successful isn't just about money, though I do like attracting it (and since money is energy, simply raising our vibration attracts more of it). It's also about success in our relationships, home lives, social lives, spiritual lives, and of course, our work lives. In fact, our work lives and the money we can make can be enhanced by our dedication to self-care.

Taking time for self-care tells the Universe that we believe we are worthy. It tells the Universe that you value yourself. Therefore, the Universe must respond by valuing you and by association, your desires. Practicing self-care means recognizing our relationship with our *self* and making this relationship a priority. Self-care requires putting in the necessary intentional effort to sustain it and calling ourselves out when we're not practicing passionate self-care.

Do you need a day off? Does your boss know? As a leader, I always made it my business to know. In fact, the number one thing anybody who's ever worked for me would say that I preached the most is that self-care and balance are critical.

I literally have had to tell my team members that were working so hard for me, "How are you? Do you need to take a day off? Do you need to take a vacation?"

I often required them to take half-day Fridays when I could tell they were especially stressed. I encouraged them to listen to the 21-day meditation by Oprah and Deepak Chopra. I recommended that they take time to journal. I planned retreats together as a team where we'd spend three days together and build our connection. We would go do yoga together, take a crystal energy class together, and of course go have spa days together. You remember, we even had matching crystal bracelets to bring in the high vibrational energy of money, success, communication, and team bonding.

I cared when they had children and were stressing themselves out so much because they weren't sitting down to have dinner with their family. I helped them structure their travel schedule to where they were only traveling two days a week and they were still knocking it out of the ballpark. I encouraged them to exercise and take care of their relationships.

Of course, this is not how corporate America works. Most corporations don't try to understand how your relationship is going, nor do they really care. They're not worried about what's happening in your life. They don't give advice on those other important aspects of employees' lives besides work-related training.

What big corps don't realize is that they will ultimately be the ones to suffer because people are not meant to live to work. It is insane to expect people to be answering emails from their boss on a Saturday night. It's so *yesterday* to continue to believe it's okay to stress out your team so much that when they do go home, they can't turn it off. Those days are over.

Burnout is real, and employees will eventually get tired of missing out on their entire lives and leave, costing the companies thousands of dollars.

For me, it was all about the whole person. I brought in coaching and leadership for the whole person. I did it instinctively, unaware of the science behind my methods at the time. Because…guess what. Self-care isn't just a pie-in-the-sky wish or executive luxury. Its benefits and value to any company's bottom line are based on scientific evidence.

No one understands the concept of self-care more than our frontline health workers. The *US National Library of Medicine Journal* article, "Caring for oneself to care for others: physicians and their self-care" written by Sandra Sanchez-Reilly, MD, MSc, Laura J. Morrison, MD, and Elise Carey, MD, et al, not only states the case for self-care being key to productivity, but it also gives several tools and strategies for doctors to practice this technique.

Their study led them to recommend improving communication and management skills through training. They recommend improving empathy along with balancing that empathy with objectivity to help them deal with losing patients. They recommend practicing self-awareness, sharing feelings, exercising, going on vacations, having hobbies, and participating in other recreation. They even promote reflective writing, practicing mindfulness and meditation, and spiritual development.

Most importantly, they encourage that health providers "prioritize personal relationships such as family and close friends," and conclude that, "…self-care has the potential not only to minimize the harm from burnout, compassion fatigue, and moral distress but to promote personal and professional well-being."

Seems like a good trade. One could also argue that this also applies to corporate work. Luckily, I'm not the only one who thinks so.

My friends over at Forbes Magazine also concur that work-life balance is an ever-evolving and important part of any healthy work environment. In fact, in Alan Kohll's March 2018 *Forbes* article, "The Evolving Definition Of Work-Life Balance," he warns of the tolls of chronic stress and workplace burnout.

Kohll spells out some of the top issues including:

- hypertension
- digestive troubles
- chronic aches and pains
- heart problems
- mental health issues due to higher risks of depression, anxiety, and insomnia
- fatigue
- mood swings
- irritability
- decreased work performance

Worse, he points out that the healthcare cost of burned-out employees is estimated to run from $125 billion to $190 billion each year in the U.S.

Kohll recommends skipping on the bean bags, coffee, and video games perks, to focus instead on paying a decent wage and offering personal growth training as well as growth within the company. He recommends extended paid maternity/paternity leave and vacation. He suggests offering a flexible work environment, flexible office hours, and remote work hours, and goes so far as to promote creating a pleasant work environment where employees feel at home while at work and enjoy their place in the company. He stresses their happiness over just working for that end-of-the-week payday.

TRY THIS to develop self-care and balance

It's easy to doubt that all this can really work in corporate America. I don't know all the answers, but I believe that we can make great changes. It's Magic!

We can start by removing all the guilt associated with self-care, especially at work, while at the same time, we integrate care for ourselves in all facets of our lives: at home, at work, in our friendships, and in other relationships. Self-care is about creating daily routines, practicing rituals, and also setting boundaries. These don't have to be extravagant days at the spa or hours spent in meditation or silence. Try any of these:

- Surround yourself with like-minded people
- Stay in bed an extra 15 minutes
- Meditate
- Let go of guilt
- Enjoy reading a good book
- Take a walk around the block with the dog
- Drive in the car with silence
- Hop on a Zoom and share a glass of wine with a friend
- Journal (see below for a few tips on journaling)
- Attend Yoga, Pilates, or any kind of exercise class, even Spin
- Spend time with your girlfriends or buddies
- Get away from the kiddos without guilt for a weekend alone or with your honey
- Say, "No" instead of "Yes"
- Go after whatever lights you up

- Get some fresh air and a good book
- Enjoy the feeling of your face in the sun for five minutes
- Lay in the grass looking up at the trees and clouds like when you were a kid
- Start your own morning coffee ritual
- Say daily affirmations
- Take a nap on a Saturday afternoon (this is my personal fave)
- Protect your energy by avoiding Energy Vampires who live off sucking out the energy of others
- Schedule and protect personal and fun times in your calendar just like you would a work meeting
- Hire a Spiritual or Intuitive Coach
- Go on Vacation!
- Oh yeah…and visit my Instagram @ManifestwithKim, and have your boss book me on a ZOOM!

We talked about journaling. Did you know journaling is an effective, even powerful practice that helps you on your path to making your dreams a reality? Here are a few journaling prompts that will enhance your ability to manifest. Try writing these down every week or so and answering each question. Keep track of your progress, and look back every now and then to see how much you're able to manifest as compared to when you first start out.

Start with these prompts:

- What am I currently grateful for that the Universe has gifted me with?
- What do I want to manifest. Why?
- What activities make me happy?
- What does my dream life look and feel like? Be very specific!
- How am I seeking healing?
- What are some practices I can begin to bring me closer to my destiny?

TOP TIP: Believe that you are worthy

1. Set aside time for yourself—find a routine that works for you.
2. Say, "no," without guilt. It's so important to honor your needs and to put the things that you need over what other people want. There's no reason to feel guilty for taking care of yourself. Boundaries, boundaries, and more boundaries. (I couldn't pronounce this word until I was 50 years old!) Learning to set boundaries is the key to not caring what others think.
3. Keep your stress in check. Know what stresses you out and make an action plan ahead of time to deal. Meditate, exercise, plan some solid, fun girl time. The options are endless!
4. Raise your Vibrations. Take time to stop and intentionally raise your vibrations. Meditation is one of the strongest ways to raise your vibes. Service is another, but only when you are giving with a completely open heart. If you're serving out of duty while feeling overwhelmed or with people who stress you out (for example, in a club or nonprofit), this is unlikely to raise your vibrations. Try making a cake for a neighbor who's having a rough day or leaving a bottle of water for your mailman. Laughter is a third powerful way to raise those vibrations. Make time to laugh and play throughout the day.
5. Create rituals that feel luxurious such as bath time with bubbles, taking a nap, or going for a walk with stillness.
6. Get moving. Find some way to move your body at least 10 minutes twice a day. Go for a walk, dance to your favorite playlist, go for a swim. You can get inspired and hit the gym (*goals!*)... Or keep it gentle. Just make sure to break a sweat and challenge yourself. Unlike what many will tell us, a little goes a long way!
7. Wash, rinse, and repeat.

And remember to listen to the signs you're receiving in your life. If you have a backache, book a massage. If you're feeling stuck in your career, hire an intuitive coach. If you're in a funk, go get a reiki session.

For a perfect example, right now as I'm writing this paragraph, I am feeling the overwhelming desire to go lie down in my ultra-comfy bed and watch *The Real Housewives*, and even though my boyfriend laughs at me, it gives me pleasure.

I'll pick back up after my nap…

NOTES

Why worry?
What is meant for you
is always meant to
find you.

Saint Lalleshwari

Chapter 8

TEN TOP TIPS FOR SUCCESS

*A*hh… I'm back from my nap, and we're nearing the end of these pages.

Before you set down this book, I'd love to give you a few tips for making your spiritual leader journey easier, faster, and more fulfilling.

Here are my top 10 secrets for becoming a badass manifesting machine:

1. **Ask for the best and the highest for all people involved in any situation.** Trust that the Universe has a hand in your interactions and in your best life. Everything happens as they should when we step into this thinking.

2. **Give yourself a break.** When you first start, it's just like starting an exercise program. You can't tear it up at the gym until you put in the time to condition your muscles. You have to start somewhere and strengthen those muscles a little each day. You start off with lighter weights, shorter distances, briefer times, and easier exercises. Each day, each week, each month you get stronger, faster, and better. But remember that it's not linear. You might see massive strides for a couple of weeks, only to have setbacks and seemingly

failures in the following weeks. But don't despair! All your cumulative work does eventually add up (or rather, it multiplies) until you're totally rocking it. That's what manifesting is.

3. **Get distracted.** If you're like most of us, you might find yourself getting thoroughly frustrated when you start meditating because of how often you get distracted. What most people don't realize is that getting distracted is one of the most important parts of the process of discovering meditation. It's your *having* to go through that discomfort and pain that allows you can gain the beauty that comes from this practice. Unfortunately, no one can predict much discomfort you might endure because it's an individual, different path for each of us. However, I can predict that your growth will be enhanced by every groan, eye roll, and every sigh uttered while trying to get back into your meditative state after a distraction. Embrace it, sister! Plus, simply noticing your distraction or your thoughts at all is a key part of meditating. The trick is to allow those thoughts to come and go, and this is what makes a successful mediation practice! And remember, Stillness is where the magical shit happens!

4. **Put your mat away!** You can't just think or meditate your way into your dream life. You can't wave a magic wand and get instant results. Manifesting requires practice. It demands that you get out of your comfort zone. Many people think that meditating will manifest their dreams. While it's nice to dream (and incredibly important), manifesting requires *action beyond meditation.* At some point, it's time to put the meditation mat away and get to work.

5. **Get started with small, deliberate actions to manifest small goals, then adjust with bigger goals and actions over time.** Take small, consistent action steps towards the goals you're setting. Practice asking for signs, even small actions (they are the basis of where true change happens, then bigger. Start with smaller, easier to attain goals. You practice with your Spiritual Tools and then one day, *poof!* You've manifested your first sign on a question you sent to the

Universe. That's how it works. You seek another sign and manifest it. Then another, and it gets easier and faster over time.

6. **Honor your pace.** It can also be quite hard to watch as others proceed at a faster pace than us. This is a no-judgment zone…be gentle with yourself. It may be helpful for you to understand that some souls come to this earth having already completed much of their work. These people are more open to following their paths and can manifest faster and more abundantly. Others have more work and lessons to learn. And we can all agree that we don't learn lessons from being successful all the time. To move forward, we must face and overcome challenges, and we also have to fail sometimes (or, in some cases, often) until we learn those lessons we need to learn.

7. **Get Zen.** Feeling flustered? Can't find your notes? Your phone? Your keys? No problem! Stop! Zen out. Take a deep breath or two. Or ten. Close your eyes if that helps (unless you're driving). Go for a quick, brisk walk. Meditate. Go into a Yoga pose. In those moments where we allow ourselves to get flustered or upset, we are slowing and sometimes even stopping the flow of the Universe. This means that any good that can come to us must work extra hard to get here. Nobody wants that! Stop and take a moment to zone out.

8. **Raise your vibration.** When you have a need or desire, or when you want to attract like-minded people to your team, to your goals, to your life, raising your vibrations is key. One of my favorite ways to raise my vibration is to actively step into being grateful. To do this, follow this procedure:

   a. Drop into your heart: Close your eyes, lay your hand at your heart, and be still.

   b. Drop deeper into your body and be grateful and thankful for whatever goes through your mind.

   c. Or you can just dance and sing a show tune at the top of your lungs! (Don't laugh it works for me!)

9. **Turn Counterclockwise.** In nature, many objects turn counterclockwise. Planets (other than Venus and Uranus) spin counterclockwise. Stars also spin counterclockwise, and even

mammal eggs in vitro spin counterclockwise more often than not during the fertilization dance. But in business, it's different. In corporate America, it's all clockwise. Sometimes, you have to practice counterintuitive ideas when you want to run a successful business. Next time everything seems to be going wrong (or you're just having a bad hair day), try literally turning yourself in a counterclockwise circle to start bringing the true flow in your life—the flow of the Universe. Just turn towards your left shoulder, and keep on turning. Unwind those blocks and open yourself up to unexpected answers and more success.

10. **Give up worrying about what other people think.** Give it up like a bad habit. Worrying about what other people think may be more hazardous for your life than some habits are for your health. It can make you unable to show your true self or silence your truth altogether. As long as you spend time worrying about what others think, you will not be able to fully live your authentic life. Remember the old saying that "it's none of my business what others think of me."

BONUS TIP: Be a Seeker!

Here's a list of many things I have done to heal, grow spiritually, and manifest. I highly recommend you use all or most of these methods to make your life the magic it is meant to be:

- Therapy
- Reiki or Energy Work
- Meditation and Stillness
- Crystal Energy Work
- Tapping
- Holographic Memory Resolution
- Ecstatic Dance
- Shaman (Acupuncture, Chanting, Drums)
- Journaling

- Traveling
- Sound Healing
- Massage
- Tarot Cards (Intuitive Healers)
- Light Language
- Vision Boards
- Spirit Guides and Angels
- Angel Numbers
- Rituals (Birthdays, New Year's Rituals, and more)
- Faith
- Trust
- Work with healers
- Astrology
- Even going to spas, detoxing, and fasting

Remember, the Universe always responds when we are in alignment.

Imagine for just a moment what a life filled with magic could be. You decide you want something, and you get it. You miss out on something only to discover that you received something even better. You feel important. Your life and work have meaning, and you're finally in a financial position to give back.

You can donate to anyone you want, whenever you want. You can support your favorite cause. The worries of the world slip away and with them, so does the stress, anxiety, fear, doubt, uncertainty, and sadness. The days are brighter, your relationships feel good and are supportive, just as you are supported by the Universe.

You have all the time in the world to play, to work, to choose which and when. You're in perfect health, at the weight you want to be, and feel fantastically in the flow!

Most of all, you give and receive love on the daily, especially to yourself. No challenge is too big, nothing is too hard. Your dreams are ripe and ready for the picking, and you are ready...*finally ready* to live the most incredible and unimaginably successful life of your wildest dreams.

And it all started with your decision to take on the life of the Corporate Hippie and apply the techniques, methods, and principles you found here in these pages. You worked hard to assimilate the magic lifestyle into your existence. You fought through the *bad* days, the *failures*, and the *disappointments* just so you could see the other side. Your accomplishments are well-earned.

Most importantly, you have learned, once and for all, that you are worthy of the best life possible. You're quickly and easily manifesting all of your magical dreams and beyond.

And why not? Think of all the great things you want, and ask yourself:

Why the F?!k *NOT* me?

******

I leave you with one last story.

It was time to make two big decisions about who was going to be editing my book (yes, this one!) and what social media team to select. I had several great candidates available for both, but I wasn't entirely clear. What was clear was that I did have two that I thought I sort of wanted to hire, but I just couldn't be sure.

I go about my business as I open myself up to answers. A friend from Dallas happens to be visiting me, and we go to the beach. No, we're not surfing the waves or sunbathing in bikinis. We're welcoming the morning with Outdoor Yoga. It's the end of class, and I'm in Savasana, the final resting pose.

I ask my Angels and my Spirit Guides to show me a sign if the two professionals that I want to hire are right for both of our best and highest. I asked to see a white feather, and then I heard in my mind, *White feather with other feathers.* Again with the crazy, magical shit that you can't make up! Because not two hours later, Susan and I wander into a boutique, and *Boom!* Like magic, those feathers are up on the wall exactly how I asked for them to appear. Staring at me is one white feather surround by lots of other feathers. I couldn't be happier with my selections!

Remember, the Universe listens when you ask. God is eagerly waiting to hear your wishes and to give them to you because you are worth it.

******

What's next?

I am so excited for your continued journey and want you to know that you are now part of my spiritual family! If you're ready to take your learning to the next level, if you're excited about the prospect of creating magic in your life, then head on over to thecorporatehippie.co. I've prepared some goodies to help you along your path. There, you can also find my podcast interviews and the link to follow my IG: @ManifestwithKim, which is filled with daily inspiration.

You can check my availability for speaking engagements and corporate workshops. I am here for you, just a click away.

My final wish is simply that you listen and remember who you are!

Now go manifest some f'ing miracles!

THE END

(or…the beginning of manifesting your journey)

Manifest like a goddess.

Kimberly Adams

ACKNOWLEDGEMENTS

It all started with you, Kim O'Hara, my book coach through two very intense VIP days where we dug deep…so deep you may remember that I once said on a podcast how much it felt like therapy. This time spent with you set up the foundation for making it to publishing this book.

Tracey Ferrin, you were the next person in my life that came in at a pivotal time and allowed me to say a resounding *YES!* to finishing my author's journey. Thank you, Tracey, for your kindness and support. Thank you for those times when you filled me with the tough love needed to get this book done. If it wasn't for the months of you *loving on* me, it most likely would have taken me another two years to get this book into the world.

This book also wouldn't have been possible without the seven fabulous years with my badass group of women at YuMe. You are now all creating magic in your lives, and I am so grateful for the spiritual family that we created together, filled with love, compassion, and trust. Ours was a beautiful time of friendship, fun, and making a ton of cash! Thank you Lynsey, Katie, Jen, Kerry, Lindsey, Lauren, Katie M., Marcee, and Rebecca!

And a huge thank you to the other key people who've been a big piece of my heart during this crazy ride…Jonathan Burks, Kate Gale, and Rebeccah Sanhueza; and thank you, Caitlin Sacks for your *absolutely stunning* cover design!

GLOSSARY

Age of Aquarius: The arrival of the Aquarian age has been associated with harmony, understanding, compassion and love. There is no firm consensus among Astrologers when it actually begins. It's best explained in the 1967 hit musical *Hair* with lyrics that describe the moon being in the seventh house and Jupiter aligning with Mars, with peace and love overseeing the planets and stars, thus marking the Age of Aquarius.

Angels: Celestial beings of love and light who can (and do) guide and assist people in all areas of life. Their work is more effective when called upon and asked for help.

Baby Seeker: This is a person with a strong desire to open up and grow spiritually. They are at the beginning of their journey. The two qualities that a Baby Seeker wants to cultivate are their ability to notice the signs around them and being open.

Body GPS: Your body's language for Yes and No answers. It's comprised of the signals that your body gives you for what's potentially healthy or not for your personal being. With practice, you can heighten your Inner Guru's (see below) ability read your Body GPS signals and determine what's good for you. Does my body want pizza or broccoli? Will this vitamin work for my body or is this vitamin better?

Corporate Hippie: It's a movement! Today's Corporate Hippie is a spiritually enlightened person who brings an evolved way of being to work. See *Lightworker* below.

Divine Timing: This is when the Universe is manifesting goals for someone at exactly the right time, place and frequency for them to receive for their ultimate best and highest expression.

Divine Light Frequency: The higher guidance that flows energetically from source, the Universe, the Infinite, God. Also known as the frequency of God.

Download: The receiving of a burst of Divine Light Frequency into one's heart and soul; this is very similar to a computer program download. It's a complete uniting with Source.

Guides or Spiritual Guides: Spiritual guides serve as the managers of a person's spiritual team. There are many types assisting us at different points in our lives.

Inner Guru: Another word for Intuition. This is your inner spiritual master that knows all the answers. It's the tingle when you turn down the wrong street. It's the voice inside urging you to take action. It's the answer that once you come to it, you realize you've known all along.

Lightworker: A lightworker is a person who is motivated to make the world a better place by elevating a higher level of consciousness for the planet. Anyone who devotes their life to being a bright light in this world could be considered a lightworker.

Magic: The result of setting powerful intentions that directly influence the course of your life in large and small ways. Magic is fueled by supernatural forces such as spirit guides, Angels and signs to illuminate your path and help you create (or *manifest*...see below) the life of your dreams.

Manifest: To cause to appear, create. To make something happen. Through regular stillness, meditation, positive thoughts and visualization aligned with actions, you can make your dreams and desires a reality. It's Magic!

Mantra: A spiritual word or expression (also called an affirmation) that is spoken aloud with the intention of creating a result. It is usually repeated to help the speaker concentrate. It can be a slogan or a motto.

Mid Seeker: Has an intense desire for spiritual growth. They have seen much tangible evidence that regular meditation and stillness for spiritual practice can make profound and sometimes unexplainable changes in their life.

Quantum Seeker: Uses multidimensional awareness in the process of discovering who they are and what their soul came here to do. Has experienced massive ability to make magic happen and manifest the shit out of their life.

Seeker: Someone who makes an honest effort to grow spiritually. There are levels including Baby Seeker, Mid Seeker, and Quantum Seeker.

Spiritual Family: This is the family that you get to create voluntarily through friends, colleagues at work, classmates, fellow club members or volunteers…the options are endless. Everyone has the distinct opportunity to build a family of choice for their best and highest expression of themselves. This family allows them to receive and operate in love, compassion and kindness.

Vibrating at a Higher Frequency: We all vibrate energy at various frequencies. The lower our frequency is, the heavier life or problems can seem. When we are vibrating at a higher frequency flow, whether intentionally or not, we will see more synchronicity within our life experiences. We also begin to see manifestation happening with more ease and less force.

RESOURCES

Enjoy this list of a few of my all-time favorite books:
- *The Universe Has Your Back* by Gabrielle Bernstein
- *You are a Badass* by Jen Sincero
- *Big Magic* by Elizabeth Gilbert
- *The Power of Now* by Eckhart Tolle
- *The Secret* by Rhonda Byrne
- *The Untethered Soul* by Michael A. Singer

The following references to cited studies, techniques, and ideas were found at the following web addresses:
- Entrepreneur.com/article/236171
- Execed.economist.com/blog/career-hacks/instincts-business-knowing-when-trust-your-gut
- Forbes.com/sites/alankohll/2018/03/27/the-evolving-definition-of-work-life-balance/?sh=16fb819e9ed3
- Gbr.pepperdine.edu/2019/08/love-the-heart-of-leadership/
- Livescience.com/amygdala.html
- Nature.com/articles/srep43456
- Ncbi.nlm.nih.gov/pmc/articles/PMC3974630/
- Ncbi.nlm.nih.gov/pmc/articles/PMC6598008/
- News.harvard.edu/gazette/story/2018/04/harvard-researchers-study-how-mindfulness-may-change-the-brain-in-depressed-patients/
- Scienceblogs.com/startswithabang/2010/10/07/counterclockwise-but-there-are#:~:text=While%20Mercury%2C%20Earth%-2C%20Mars%2C,planets%20stand%20out%20as%20weirdos
- Sonorrari.com/single-post/2017/04/06/10-Big-Companies-That-Promote-Employee-Meditation

- Spglobal.com/_division_assets/images/special-editorial/iif-2019/whenwomenlead_.pdf
- Spglobal.com/en/
- Thebrain.mcgill.ca/flash/d/d_04/d_04_cr/d_04_cr_peu/d_04_cr_peu.html#:~:text=Each%20amygdala%20is%20located%20close,it%20causes%20in%20the%20body.
- The Secret, by Rhonda Byrne
- Quoteinvestigator.com/2019/06/20/spiritual/

Intention + Action = Magic

Kimberly Adams

BEFORE YOU GO...

Before you go...

We are just getting started with this incredible Corporate Hippie Movement and would love for you to join us. Remember, I am here for anything and everything you need to get going on your journey.

Ways to connect:
Instagram: @ManifestwithKim
Facebook: @KimberlyAdams
LinkedIn: @Kimberly Adams
Clubhouse: @ManifestwithKim
www.thecorporatehippie.co

I would love to be a part of your podcast, radio show, or TV spot. We can book a speaking engagement in person or on Zoom! Shoot me a note to info@thecorporatehippie.co and let's get your team manifesting the profits, work environment, and community impact that your business is destined to give.

Breathe...
Breathe...
Breathe...

Made in the USA
Las Vegas, NV
03 June 2021